Finding Authentic Hope & Wholeness

Finding Authentic Hope & Wholeness

5 QUESTIONS THAT WILL

change YOUR LIFE

DR. KATHY KOCH

MOODY PUBLISHERS
CHICAGO

Edited by Ali Childers
Interior design: Ragont Design
Cover design: Rule 29

Library of Congress Cataloging-in-Publication Data

Koch, Kathy.
    Finding authentic hope and wholeness : five questions that will change your life / Kathy Koch.
        p. cm.
    Includes bibliographical references and index.
    ISBN 978-0-8024-0282-0
    1. Identification (Religion) 2. Identity (Psychology)—Religious aspects—Christianity. 3. Self-confidence—Religious aspects—Christianity. I. Title.

BV4509.5.K63 2005
248.4—dc22

2004020513

5 7 9 10 8 6 4

Printed in the United States of America

I dedicate Finding Authentic Hope and Wholeness
to my triune God.

*I'm grateful to God the Father
for creating me and loving me unconditionally.
I'm honored He has given me gifts to use for His purposes,
and I pray that He is glorified through the ideas presented here.
I'm especially grateful for His wisdom and truth.*

*I'm grateful to Jesus, my Lord and Savior,
for willingly taking the punishment for my sins upon Himself
and dying so I can live with Him forever after my time on earth is done.
I'm especially grateful that He is my peace and joy.*

*I'm grateful to the Holy Spirit for guiding me
to understand God's Word and will.
I'm especially grateful that He empowers me to obey.*

CONTENTS

ACKNOWLEDGMENTS

I'M THANKFUL TO GOD: Father, Son, and Holy Spirit. God's presence in my life is truly life-changing and enriching. Without Him, I would have had no desire to write this book or ability to do so. I owe Him everything.

My gratitude to my entire family runs deep. I'm sorry my dad didn't live long enough to read this book. I think he would have liked it. I'm grateful my mom is still a significant part of my life. Her support is a consistent blessing. Their loving parenting is a great example. I was also heavily influenced by my grandparents. My mom's parents are among my heroes. Additionally, I value the love and strength I receive from my brother, Dave, his wife, Debbie, and their three children, Betsy, Katie, and Andy.

Board members from Celebrate Kids, Inc. have believed in me and the message of the Model of Authentic Hope and Wholeness for years. I'm better for knowing them, and Celebrate Kids, Inc. is healthier because of their involvement. Ron Horton, Andrea Heitz, Mark Davis, Timmie Mosley, Edra Hudson, Linda Currier, and Jack Shreffler are God's choice servants.

The men and women who work with me at Celebrate Kids, Inc. add to my joy and allow me to accomplish so much more than I could without them. And that's an understatement! Joyce Penninger, Toni Gerhard, Linda Depler, Tina Hollenbeck, Denice Crawford, Sharon May, Angela Bunyard, Martin Critz, Sandra Critz, and Rachael D'Angelo are unselfish, wise, fun, encouraging, and very valuable. Also, Kevin Schreiber (our webmaster), Karl Giere (our graphic artist), and Lori Cable (our grant writer) have been used by God to strengthen our efforts. I'm grateful for this entire team.

I've been privileged to be a part of some healthy churches through the years. Ever since moving to Fort Worth, I've been a member of Grace Community Bible Church. My pastor, Ron Horton, and many others have supported me, taught me a great deal, and helped pray this book into existence. I'll be forever grateful.

God has surrounded me with some vibrant mentors. I don't have words that adequately communicate the depth of my gratitude to them. They know what they've done to help my development and that of this message. Chip Griepsma, Andrea Heitz, Linda Page, Dave Roever, Brad Sargent, and Pat Titsworth—you make a positive difference in my life. (I'm also grateful for Mordecai. He, too, has taught me much.)

Bekah and Mike Mulvaney hosted some friends and me for several writing retreats where the possibility of writing this book was first investigated. They were invaluable. And I owe a big "thank you" to editors of several magazines who asked me to write articles and regular columns for them. Because of them, I gained confidence and skill as a writer. I'm especially grateful to Jill Briscoe, Shelly Esser, and the *Just Between Us* family.

I'm grateful for every person who has hired me to speak and for people in audiences throughout the world who have been used by God to strengthen my ideas. They have taught me much as they reacted to my content and raised excellent questions.

Through the years, many have contributed to Celebrate Kids, Inc., which has allowed us to keep going during some lean times. Because of their faith in God and in our work, this book was completed.

I'm grateful to people who allowed me to tell their stories within these pages and on our Web site. I don't take their trust lightly. Their willingness to be a part of my teaching humbles me.

God used Nancy Elwood, the executive director of SHARE Education Services of Budapest, Hungary, in a significant way. She recommended me to speak at a conference sponsored by Moody Bible Institute. It's because of connections made there that this book exists. I'll always be grateful.

Working with people from Moody Publishers has been a very positive experience. I can say the same thing for Moody Bible Institute, Moody Radio, and Moody Conferences. I'm honored to be affiliated with them, and I'm glad our ministry will continue beyond this first book. I'm especially grateful to God for Dr. Joseph Stowell, Jim Jenks, Mark Tobey, Elsa Mazon, and Ali Childers. And I appreciate everyone from the marketing and publicity departments, as their work assures more people will be influenced by this book. That's why I wrote it. Not to be an author, but to have a greater influence. I'm glad I can partner with Moody toward that goal.

INTRODUCTION

THIS BOOK IS DESIGNED to help you make sure that your core needs are met in healthy ways. When they are, you will be secure and competent. You'll also know who you are, whom you "fit" with, and why you're alive. As a result, you'll be at peace.

Everyone has the same God-given basic needs—security, identity, belonging, purpose, and competence. That's what this book is about— these needs and unhealthy and healthy ways people go about trying to meet them and what God has to say about them. I pray that this material will positively affect you as you rely on God's help to put these ideas into practice—in all areas of your life. Are you a wife or husband? Use the principles to strengthen your marriage. Are you a mom or dad? Use the ideas to better parent your child(ren). Are you a daughter or son? (That's a trick question. Of course you are!) Use the truths when relating to your parents. I expect you'll also apply the concepts in these pages to your friendships and relationships with coworkers, clients, and others you serve.

I have developed what I call the Model of Authentic Hope and Wholeness to lead us to practical answers to some of life's most relevant questions. Through this Model, we'll learn the difference between authentic answers and inadequate quick fixes, real reasons and seductive counterfeits, trustworthy truths and outright lies. I believe this Model provides you with many ways to celebrate all the people God has connected you with. To God be the glory!

ONE

ROCK BOTTOM OR ANCHORED TO THE ROCK?

VIVID, EARLY MEMORIES often capture the essence of how we look at life—for better or for worse. Even at six years old, fitting in was important to me. It was so important that, one day after first grade, I sat down in the middle of my parents' bed and announced to my mom, "I don't want to be tall or clumsy anymore!" Both my clumsiness and my height made me stand out. I tripped over things that weren't there and ran into things that were. I couldn't hide in a crowd. I squirmed when I caught children and adults staring at me.

My mom heard my heart's cry. She didn't proclaim, "Well, get over it, you're going to be tall!" Instead, she talked with my dad about it, and they realized I had a perceived weakness that could be changed (my clumsiness) and one that couldn't (my height).

You know what they did? They problem solved. I praise God they were solution-focused parents! They enrolled me in dance class, and I thrived! Through tap and ballet, I quickly overcame my clumsiness. Because of my height, I was the center of the back row—which I decided was a position of high honor! (When a perceived weakness is an unchangeable characteristic, changing one's attitude toward it is the next best thing.)

Be a solution focused person.

Perhaps you can relate to my need to belong, even if your circumstances weren't anything like mine. I believe belonging is one of our core needs, created by God. This book is about meeting the needs of security, identity, belonging, purpose, and competence in healthy ways so we can experience the hope and wholeness that God desires for us.

I'll mention many healthy and unhealthy ways that these needs can be fulfilled and how the hope that results can be either authentic or counterfeit. I'll illustrate this first with my dance story. My parents' solution positively affected my belonging. I fit in with other dancers and became more comfortable with my height. My other four significant core needs were fulfilled too:

Core Need #1: Security
Who can I trust?
I can trust my parents because they solved my problem.
I can trust myself because I no longer trip over things.

Core Need #2: Identity
Who am I?
I am a tall dancer who is no longer clumsy.

Core Need #3: Belonging
Who wants me?
The other dancers want me.
They don't have a problem with my height.

Core Need #4: Purpose
Why am I alive?
I'm alive to dance!

Core Need #5: Competence
What do I do well?
I tap-dance well.

At the age of six, those were my answers. I anchored myself to them to meet my basic needs. I was satisfied.

I lived for Fridays, when dance lessons took place after school. I even assisted the teacher when I was too old for lessons in her class. Years later, I taught tap after school to many second- and third-grade girls. I wanted to share some of the blessings I'd received. I still have vivid, positive memories of those afternoons and year-end recitals!

As I hope you can see from the Model's questions and answers, one solution can meet all five needs. Since I was a tall child and uncomfortable with my height, my primary desire was to fit in (belonging). Once I did, I was able to positively view the unchangeable attribute of my height (identity). Dancing gave me purpose, and the more dance lessons I took, the more competent I became.

My need for security was also met. Not only did I appreciate how much I could trust my parents to solve problems with and for me, but I could trust myself more because I was no longer clumsy. I also knew I could trust the other dancers and my beloved dance teacher, Miss Lafaye.* They didn't laugh at my height. My security became broad based. All it took was my parents' act of enrolling me in dance lessons to constructively take care of all five of my core needs.

Are my danced-based answers to the Model's questions relevant to my life today? Absolutely. If I had questioned my body image (part of the *Who am I?* identity question) even a little longer, I might not be able to stand in front of large crowds as a public speaker like I do today. Also, if I had continued to view my height negatively, that toxic point of view might have seeped over into other areas. I would not be who I am today if I'd been allowed to grow up negative and pessimistic. So even the "little" decisions can make a big difference.

Although the core needs and their questions remain the same throughout life, our answers change as we mature and take responsibility for ourselves. Growth results in more rock-solid answers and a sharpened sense of direction for the future, as I'll explain later.

*Names have been changed, except for family members and coworkers at Celebrate Kids, Inc.

PERCEPTION IS NINE-TENTHS OF THE PROBLEM

I admit that it's easier now to maintain a positive attitude about my height than when I was a child. Even though I became comfortable with my height through dance lessons, I didn't view it as a strength. I just thought I was tall because my parents were tall. I never dreamed God might have a purpose for it. As an adult, it's been exciting to discover that He did!

For instance, when I taught second graders, I could hang art projects from the ceiling without using a ladder. This made things easier for me—and my coworkers. They could come get me instead of the ladder stored at the other end of the building! But that wasn't the only benefit.

If you've flown overseas, you know how high the overhead bins are for carry-on bags on those big planes. I have no trouble lifting bags in and out of those spaces. My first flight overseas was from Los Angeles, California, to Taipei, Taiwan, on my way to Manila in the Philippines to speak at a conference for teachers at Christian schools. Can you picture me—all six foot one of me—on a plane with people heading to Asia? I'll never forget the look of desperation on the faces of the Asians who smiled at me and pointed to their suitcases after I easily put my suitcase in the overhead bin. I knew what they wanted me to do! And I did it, getting stronger with every bag.

Since I'm a public speaker, there's at least one other professional advantage to my height. Audience members can see me, even if I'm standing behind a podium on the same level as their seats. That's not what makes me an effective speaker, but it helps that I can see everyone and they can see me.

God makes no mistakes. He has reasons for creating each person with certain attributes. Every person you know is a unique "package deal," an unrepeatable miracle, not an accident in a meaningless society. The same is true about you. Absolutely. Learning to actively discern the truths about our strengths is part of what makes hope and wholeness *authentic.* Without knowing what is true about God and who He's made us to be, we can find ourselves passively wallowing in our weaknesses or submerging ourselves in sin.

My height contributes positively to God's complete plan—involving more than just my legitimate childhood identity of being the center of the back row. I'm glad I've lived long enough to understand that God intentionally and purposefully equipped me. Even though I view my height as a strength, it's not the source of my security (the first need). That would be foolish. How would people taller than I am affect me?

Later I came to realize that I was someone who could use words well and who found joy in both talking and reading (shaping the second need for identity). These characteristics helped me acquire the nickname "Chatty Kathy." My mom remembers her mother first calling me that when I was about three years old. This love of communication affected my belonging (the third need) and purpose (the fourth need), because I participated in community theater from a young age and joined the forensics (speech) team when I was in high school.

I don't believe it was an accident that I became a teacher of second graders who emphasized literacy. Nor was it by chance that my doctoral studies in reading and educational psychology were also a good fit. Usually I have dictionaries, thesauruses, and concordances within an arm's reach. (The plurals aren't mistakes. One volume of each is not enough!)

Do you see how my identity, belonging, and purpose provided the internal mind-set for external, public competence (the fifth need)? Realizing my strengths of speaking and reading (part of my identity) led to my belonging in theater and forensics and part of my purpose, which was to speak well and get the theater parts. I was motivated and equipped to gain competence. My competence increased my positive sense of security (our first need), which demonstrates the circular, looping-back effect of the linkages between this Model's five components (i.e., five core needs). Directors and teachers who proved themselves trustworthy also influenced my security. They pointed out my strengths, influencing my identity and overall sense of wholeness.

If my need for security had not been met, eventually the rest wouldn't have held up. They would have tumbled down like a house of cards. Security forms the base of the Model of Authentic Hope and

Wholeness. If security is not met and strong in healthy ways, our other needs will remain at least partially unmet. Although I could have attempted to meet this need through my height and ability to communicate, I wouldn't have been successful. (The best answer to our security question involves a *who* not a *what*.) Not surprisingly, people made the difference. I knew I could trust my coaches and teachers. My parents helped me rehearse and eagerly attended performances. I sensed their support and approval, both when I did well and when I didn't. Therefore, I could continue investing in my activities, and none of my core needs went unmet.

So this tall one who chatted in school now earns a living by writing and standing to speak. God is good! And I have no doubt that He has excellent things in the future for you, no matter your past or present circumstances. I choose to believe this for children, too, which is why I also teach young people this Model. Does this ring true in your heart, or does it feel impossible right now to believe God has designed a positive future for you and the people you love? Either way, stick with me to see why I believe what I do. We'll get there.

AUTHENTIC HOPE AND WHOLENESS

Answering the five life questions according to my involvement with dance worked well for a while. For example, you might remember that the question representing our belonging need is, *Who wants me?* When I was a dancer, I could answer that in this way: "The other dancers do. They don't have a problem with my height." But what happened when I no longer danced regularly?

Maybe you have experienced a shift in your answers to the life questions. Perhaps that's been the result of positive growth over time, like my shift from dancing to forensics. Or perhaps it wasn't so constructive. Your needs were met for a while, then you felt unsatisfied. You got involved in something new and had fewer needs for a while, and then you again floundered. Are you or people you know living in this kind of unstable reality?

I think all people want their needs met. And who wouldn't like a permanent fix for their basic needs? Unless we've already given up, we're all looking for hope. However, some people don't understand their core needs, so they're asking the wrong questions and looking in the wrong places for answers. That leads them to find only false, temporary, counterfeit solutions that don't really satisfy. They're synthetic impersonations, not built upon the reality and truth of what really does satisfy. False hope and wholeness may result in even more despair than we knew before our search for solutions began. Ultimately, these counterfeits won't help and they won't last. They will disappoint us. And once again, people hooked on what's false soon believe there's nothing to count on. But there is a true, permanent, authentic source for hope and wholeness!

You know what made the difference for me? Actually, I should reword that. Do you know *who* made the difference for me? Jesus Christ, God's Son. How did that difference happen? I humbled myself by accepting that I'd always be inadequate on my own. I saw my needs and, thankfully, drew the conclusion that I was in need of a Savior and that Jesus was the One. He is my Authentic Hope. My needs didn't change after anchoring my life to Jesus as my Rock. I still needed security, identity, belonging, purpose, and competence, just as I do today. The life questions didn't change. But my living answers did. God met all five of my core needs, resulting in authentic wholeness. He was the permanent, rock-solid answer, and He still is. I've stopped floundering. Have you?

I've used a lot of my story to illustrate these principles. What I'd like to do now is summarize the basics of the Model of Authentic Hope and Wholeness so we're on the same page before forging ahead. We'll revisit these concepts many times and apply them to our lives and those of others. I've prayed that God will illuminate your mind and heart through this Model and use its life-changing material to bring you authentic hope and wholeness. Ready? Let's go!

Hope

Everyone is looking for hope—that unshakable, rock-solid, confident expectation of things to come. Authentic hope is established when our number one foundational need of security is fulfilled in a personal relationship with God the Father, through choosing to anchor ourselves and our lives to His Son, Jesus Christ.

Authentic hope expects God to work redemptive good out of life's rubble as we seek, discover, and love Him. Authentic hope is affirmed repeatedly in our souls when we learn from firsthand experiences and God's Word that God is who He says He is and that He makes no empty promises. When we have a secure relationship with God, we have a twofold hope: (1) hope for eternal life, since after we die we'll be in heaven with our Savior, and (2) hope for victorious resolution of life's challenges, frustrations, and failures because Jesus Christ is not only Savior but also Lord of life.

Before going any further, let's define authentic hope:

> *Authentic hope* is an unshakable, rock-solid confidence established in a personal relationship with God, the Father, through faith in Jesus Christ and, therefore, salvation from our sins. This is affirmed in our souls as we learn through experience and His Word that God is worthy of our confidence.

> *The LORD is good to those whose hope is in him,*
> *to the one who seeks him.*
> *–Lamentations 3:25*

> *Christ in you [is] the hope of glory!*
> *–Colossians 1:27*

Wholeness

Everyone is looking for wholeness—a genuine, real, energizing integration of answers to the classic questions of all time: *Who am I?* and *Why am I here?* Scripture, research, and the testimonies of many clearly show that authentic wholeness involves more than these two classic questions. Authentic wholeness occurs only when our five core needs are fulfilled in Jesus Christ. Trying to meet our needs in anyone or anything other than Him can result in a temporary or shallow sense of wholeness, but not long-lasting or authentic, real, actual, legitimate, true, genuine wholeness.

There are reasons why I structured this model in its particular order: (#1) Security: *Who can I trust?* (#2) Identity: *Who am I?* (#3) Belonging: *Who wants me?* (#4) Purpose: *Why am I alive?* and (#5) Competence: *What do I do well?* While all the needs are connected to and affected by each other, I've seen more complete wholeness take place in people's lives when they have a place to start from (security, in this Model) and then follow a progression that makes sense (all the way to competence).

If you haven't thought through the Model's questions before (or it's been a while), I suggest that you follow along with this order since I am certain that each component is specially connected to the ones between which it is bordered, or sandwiched. All the needs are still connected to and affected by each other, but I've found that this progression is helpful to many who work through it, and I hope you're willing to give it a shot. The key to wholeness is that *all* five needs are met, and, ultimately, met through Christ.

WATCH OUT FOR COUNTERFEITS!

There are at least three ways we can deceive ourselves as we seek to meet our needs. We can:

> confuse wants with needs,
> ask misleading questions, and/or
> attempt to meet needs in unhealthy ways.

Confusing Wants with Needs

We can confuse wants with authentic needs. Have you ever declared, "I need coffee!"? Unless you were actually dying of thirst, you didn't need coffee; you wanted some. How many children say they need to go to the movies? What about our need for happiness, cool friends, smart children, more money, or more _____? (You fill in the blank.) What have you heard yourself say recently? Was it a need or a want? Authentic needs involve life-or-death issues. Without them attained, we die physically, emotionally, intellectually, socially, and/or spiritually. Wants only parade themselves as matters of life and death.

Asking Misleading Questions

We can easily be tricked, because wrong questions disguise themselves cleverly. Asking, "*What* can I trust?" causes trouble every time. Things fade away, so putting security in things is dangerous. Beauty, fame, fortune, position, academic grades, dancing ability—none of these last forever. It is better to ask, "*Who* can I trust?" The only answer for authentic security is Jesus Christ.

Attempting to Meet Needs in Unhealthy Ways

We can wrongly anchor ourselves to unreliable and inaccurate answers and use unhealthy methods to find answers that suit us. For instance, in regard to the core need of competence, the pivotal question is, *What do I do well?* Have you ever needed to feel competent so badly that you cheated while playing cards or golf or in school when your teacher wasn't looking? Eventually, when we attempt to meet needs in unhealthy ways, the lies catch up with us. Pain and trouble often follow. In the previous illustration, cheating may result in feeling competent, but not in a true state of competence. We may be known as skilled cardplayers, talented golfers, or bright students. We're not, though. Perhaps we really could be, but we'll never know because we cheat. Either way, the lie wins. Ultimately, we lose.

The Results

These counterfeit errors in judgment may produce results that look like authentic hope and wholeness. However, they will not last because they are built on lies. What do these principles look like in a person's life? Let me share a slice-of-life story about my friend Emily.

Emily: From Rock Bottom to Rock Solid

Although physically present, Emily's mother was emotionally absent. Emily gave up trying to relate to her when she was still a young girl. Therefore, the relationship Emily shared with her dad became very important to her. Even though he wasn't very involved in her life either, Emily noticed he did pay atten-

tion when she brought home perfect papers and straight A's. He also went to every band concert.

Emily's dad only recognized her competence (#5). The older Emily grew, the more clearly she understood from his comments and behaviors that only perfect performances mattered to him. Being perfect and earning her dad's approval became so important to Emily that she didn't say a thing to anyone about the ways he sexually abused her. Also, like many abused girls, she didn't know at the time that such sexual behaviors between adults and children were wrong. Once she understood it was wrong, she feared telling anyone. She was sure if she told anyone and her father found out, then she wouldn't be "daddy's perfect girl" anymore. And then who would she be? That was her only identity (#2). Emily desperately wanted a healthy relationship with her dad (belonging, #3). All she knew was an unhealthy one, and at that age it was hard for her to know the difference.

Because of her dad's priorities and expectations, Emily was trying to meet all five wholeness needs through her competence (#5), meaning perfection *in her mind. That's the grave danger in perfectionism—perfectionists are conditioned to believe that only perfection is good enough. Imagine how Emily felt and related to others while growing up with these beliefs:*

Security: What (not who) can I trust? *My excellent grades; I earn A's.*

Identity: Who am I? *I'm an A student.*

Belonging: Who wants me? *My dad notices me when I earn A's.*

Purpose: Why am I alive? *I need to make Dad proud and have him notice me by earning A's.*

Competence: What do I do well? *I earn A's.*

Since Emily was trying to answer the life questions through her competence (#5), all five answers evaporated when she earned her one-and-only C. Overnight she went from having a strong sense of what Martin Luther King Jr. called "somebody-ness," to "nobodyness."[1] She had nothing to be secure in (#1) and no identity (#2). She believed she had no one to belong to (#3), no reason to exist (purpose, #4), and, supposedly, she did nothing well (competence, #5).

I've met many teenagers and adults who tell me that they feel this way, like "no one with nothing." Some give up trying once they determine they can't be perfect anymore. Their past failures negate hope for tomorrow and shatter hope and wholeness in the present. When competence (#5) is all they strive for, they end up with nothing when they "fail."

Emily went all the way through school, including college, earning just one C in college calculus. Would it surprise you to hear that Emily lied to her parents about the grade? First, she told them the grades weren't posted. Eventually she said she earned a B. Not only that, Emily didn't tell me about the grade until I was writing this chapter—and we've been close friends and confidants for seventeen years! Emily admitted she felt like such a complete failure that she was suicidal. As a result of this one C, she changed majors to one she believed would be less demanding academically.

When Emily first went off to college, she struggled because her dad's evaluation, on which she had become so dependent, was no longer directly available to her. Then the C grade, lying about it, and changing majors further distanced her from her family. Before the C, all her basic needs for wholeness were met—though met in unhealthy ways. After the C, none of them were fulfilled.

Emily didn't totally give up, but she faced many more struggles. Her perfectionistic, performance mind-set and her high need for approval resulted in continued stress, so much so that she developed an eating disorder. How unfortunate! Emily, her husband, and her Christian counselor believe this was a

*direct result of her dad's abuse and valuing her for competence
(#5) rather than for the woman God created her to be.*

*Emily struggled, even after she became a Christian and
turned her life over to God. She learned that authentic hope—
anchoring yourself and your life securely in Jesus—doesn't
guarantee quick fixes to major problems or a smooth, effortless
path to authentic wholeness. It has taken her a long time to
put off her old ways of thinking. Through Bible study, discipleship, worship, and counseling, Emily has learned to change her
mind-set and trust God to meet all five basic needs, resulting
in authentic wholeness. Watching her develop the following
truthful beliefs has been a privilege and joy:*

Security: Who (not what) can I trust? *God has proven
Himself faithful. I can depend on Him to love me even when
I'm not perfect.*

Identity: Who am I? *I am a child of God, saved by grace!
I am so valuable to God that He sent His Son, Jesus Christ, to
die for me even though I'm imperfect. And I am more than my
performances.*

Belonging: Who wants me? *God wants me, and I want
Him to be a part of my life. I don't have to earn God's love or
do anything special to have Him pay attention to me. This is
also true of my relationship with my husband and a few trusted friends. It's getting easier to think of God as my Father.*

Purpose: Why am I alive? *I want to glorify God in who I
am and all I do. This includes my health and body image.*

Competence: What do I do well? *God is becoming my
source of strength and wisdom. Therefore, I'm learning to turn
my struggles over to Him and rely on the Holy Spirit's power
day by day. And when I don't feel very competent, it's okay because God is my foundation, and He is more than competent.
He's the One who is perfect.*

Did you notice how Emily based her new set of beliefs on realistic assessments and truths, instead of faulty assessments and lies? What a difference there is between her lists now that she's developed authentic hope (confidence in Jesus Christ) and authentic wholeness (all five needs met in God)! I'm confident Emily will mature in these areas as she progresses through life.

A personal, dynamic, and complete relationship with God the Father through His Son, Jesus Christ, is the core of the Model. I believe we must all grow in our ability to rely on God. This can be difficult initially for those who, like Emily, have personally experienced deep pain or believe tomorrow is uncertain. Whether we are new believers, mature Christians, or people searching for what to believe, personal knowledge of God and following Him are the keys to meeting all five needs and experiencing authentic hope and wholeness.

Trust in the LORD forever, for the LORD,
the LORD, is the Rock eternal.
–Isaiah 26:4

· ·

BUILDING
—ON—
THE ROCK

What do you think about what you've read so far? How does it strike you? How do you currently answer the five basic questions? You may want to write your answers here or on a separate piece of paper:

Security: *Who can I trust?*
Identity: *Who am I?*
Belonging: *Who wants me?*

Purpose: *Why am I alive?*
Competence: *What do I do well?*

> ‣ *Did you feel like leaving any of them blank? Why?*
> ‣ *Are you satisfied with how your basic needs are being met? Why or why not?*
> ‣ *At this point in your life, is meeting one need more important than meeting another?*

Taking time to answer these questions now will enhance your understanding and application of this information on authentic hope and wholeness. Your answers will also create a baseline to look back on as you read further.

TWO

CHUTES AND LADDERS LINKAGES

THE BETTER WE UNDERSTAND the components and structure of this framework, the deeper we'll be able to go to make positive changes in our own lives. Understanding the system as a whole will help us gain more from the chapters that follow as well as have richer interactions with our peers and protégés whom we mentor.

In this chapter, we'll focus on the interconnected relationships among the five core needs, the danger of leaving any need out, and how we can use the Model for problem solving. Here are our five core needs, their corresponding questions, and brief life-changing answers:

Security: Who can I trust? *I can trust God. He does not lie, His Word is true, He is always able and available to help, and He forgives me and loves me no matter what.*

Identity: Who am I? *I'm someone God loves whom Jesus Christ died for!*

Belonging: Who wants me? *Because of my faith in Jesus Christ, I belong to God. He wants me because of who He is, not because of what I do.*

Purpose: Why am I alive? *I am alive to glorify God through who I am and through what I do. Keys to this are becoming more like Christ* *through a relationship with Him, loving God well, loving my neighbor as myself, spreading the good news of the gospel, and helping Christians mature in their faith.*

Competence: What do I do well? *I can do anything well God asks me to do with His strength, power, energy, love, and wisdom working in me through the Holy Spirit.*

When our foundational core need for security (#1) is met in Christ, our identity (#2) can be found in God, and we can truly know who we are. It flows from this that we belong (#3) to Him forever, our purpose (#4) is to glorify Him, and He is all we need in order to be competent (#5).

The concept of universal human needs is nothing particularly new. A person's list of needs—general or core needs—is likely to find roots in the five components in the Model of Authentic Hope and Wholeness. You may wonder what makes this model any different.

Three things. First, all the needs are linked, and a person's wholeness is affected by each component. Second, God isn't typically included as the Creator or Fulfiller in models highlighting similar needs, but He is central to this Model. Third, the dynamic nature of the integration among the needs allows the Model to serve as a practical problem-solving tool for children, teens, and adults.

In the next section, we'll examine details related to the sequence. Then we'll look at what God brings to the Model. I'll share some about how I developed this Model and address its problem-solving nature.

A DYNAMIC AND COMPLETE SEQUENCE

I think I've made a sound case that our basic needs are linked in a dynamic system. This is why authentic hope (security anchored in Christ, #1) can be increasingly authenticated and strengthened as the other four needs are clearly, deliberately, and rightly met as we let God and His Word work in us.

The linkages among our core needs indicate that when one need is met in healthy ways, the prospect of the others being met in healthy ways increases. It's also true that when one need is met in unhealthy ways, our other needs will most likely become tainted with toxins as well. Each component is so responsive to the others that, even when we make a small change, many parts of our lives are affected (for good or bad) depending on the nature of that change.

For example, do you know any children who are temporarily very successful academically (competence, #5)? They may do well in the eighth grade, but not ninth. Or perhaps they begin the school year well, but later their grades slide. These types of "chute" experiences often occur because children lack purpose (#4). Their academic abilities can satisfy them for a while. They might do well just because they like learning or because certain relationships are influential (belonging, #3). But not having their need for purpose met (*Why am I alive?*), causes competence to eventually fall.

The movement through the Model's components reminds me of the delightful children's game Chutes and Ladders. The goal of this game is to move upward on the ladders to reach the treasure—but not land on a spot where you end up sliding down those chutes! Similarly, in the Model, if we try to go through life without all five needs met, we'll find ourselves hitting a snag that drops us down to take care of the needs we skipped. (Sometimes the drop is really painful, isn't it!) After sliding down the chutes, if we don't give up and quit, we'll land on ladders again. We'll eventually reach the treasure as long as we keep playing. It's the same with this Model. When we keep wanting and searching for more from life—for authentic hope and wholeness—most of us will learn how to have our needs successfully fulfilled.

The "secret" of the sequence of needs is something I discovered in my early days of research into people's core needs. At first when my university colleagues and I taught about these needs, we presented the components in a different order and something felt "off."[1] The sequence's order as it stands today is easier for people to work through and more effective when problem-solving.

HOW GOD MEETS OUR FIVE CORE NEEDS

The previous section addressed the reality that any one component can have a constructive or destructive influence on the others.

Because the needs are integrated and responsive, what happens to one component will influence the others. Following the Model's sequence provides an intentional path toward wholeness. What this section shows is how rooting the sequence in God is the only way to bring biblically authentic wholeness into the picture.

When my colleagues and I taught public school educators about the five core needs, it was apparent to me that the sequence wasn't the only thing "off." Even though our approach genuinely helped people, God had been left out of the equation.

The Lord used these seminars to show me how dangerous it is to try to meet God-created core needs without Him. As I taught, I was convicted of my own need to turn completely to Him and away from things that can fade away like knowledge and reputation. Therefore, I studied His Word to determine if these were in fact core needs designed by Him to be met primarily in Him.[2] He showed me that they are, through my studies and discussions with mentors and Christian leaders whom I respect.

When we place our faith in God's Son, Jesus Christ, we can know beyond knowledge that we can wholeheartedly trust God (security, #1). Then we are better able to understand, believe, and respect who we are in Christ (identity, #2). Knowledge about ourselves in Christ (e.g., we are forgiven and purified when we confess our sins—1 John 1:9) assures us of our place in His kingdom and meets our need for belonging (#3). We experience His acceptance and know we can continue approaching Him with confident assurance (Hebrews 4:16).

There are other authentic connections too. Knowing God will never leave or forsake us (Deuteronomy 31:6) influences both belonging (#3—He wants us) and security (#1—we can trust Him; He's there for us). What about purpose (#4)? Is it also connected to security? Yes. Our security increases when we discover that God trusts us enough to give us worthwhile and valuable purposes (Ephesians 2:10). (There are many other attributes, Scriptures, and relationships we could include, but these hopefully give you an idea of the interconnectedness of needs.)

There is also a link between the last wholeness need (competence,

#5) and the first (security, #1). The more we learn to rely upon and see God as our competence (John 15:5), the more secure we will become in Him as our firm, unfailing, ever-present, unmovable Rock. And reversing the direction, the more we choose to trust God (security), the more we believe He is our competence.

I trust the interconnectedness of our five core needs is becoming clearer as we go along. They're all linked and each one influences the others. Do notice, though, that without having our security (#1) met in a trustworthy God through faith in Christ, nothing else has a solid foundation. Although we may not always enter a change process at the "natural" beginning stage of security, we must eventually know who we can trust. Without our security well established in Christ, our other four needs can't be met in entirely healthy ways.

Let's continue our exploration of linkages in the Model, but this time with another friend of mine, Dominick. You may want to especially watch for what happens when his legitimate needs finally get met in authentic ways. (If you remember back to chapter 1, Emily's story showed us what can happen when we try to meet legitimate needs in counterfeit ways.)

Dominick: Changed Identity, Changed Life

"I don't usually work with other people, but I think you'll be helpful." Lillian's statement of her confidence in Dominick revolutionized the way he thought about himself. It almost instantly changed his identity.

In 1983, Dominick volunteered to help a well-educated woman edit a book she was writing. Not expecting too much from Dominick, but open to the possibility that God wanted her to work with him, she handed Dominick the entire four-hundred-page manuscript and told him to come back in a week with suggestions for restructuring the content into a manageable and comprehensible book. To her surprise, he did just that. Her words of confidence in him further affirmed and influenced Dominick.

Because of chronic illness, up until this point Dominick

had worked only four hours each day in a menial job that was unrelated to his advanced training. He admits to being depressed and having low expectations for his future, even though several years earlier he graduated with honors from college with a degree in linguistics.

Lillian invested in Dominick and trained him while they worked on several other book projects together. As she affirmed and influenced Dominick, his sense of security was altered. In addition to security in God (his authentic hope), he was now able to have some security in others because of this positive and trusting relationship, thus fortifying his authentic hope. Encouraged by her honest feedback and helpful instruction, Dominick learned to trust himself, which further met his need for security. His expanded security allowed him to believe in his new identity as a valued editor and writer.

Dominick's new skills eventually led him to a position as a resource writer for an international ministry where I met him in 1994. After several years of successful contributions there, he moved on to an excellent position at a seminary as a resource writer, conference planner, and mentor to students and faculty in his areas of expertise. This move was possible because Dominick invited four friends, who knew him well and in different capacities, to help him answer questions like, What's next? Where do I go from here? What are my strengths? Who am I? In just a few years he matured from being a man with only a few trusted friends, who was drifting and saw no future for himself, to one who belonged and was asking others to help him determine his next best steps in discovering God's purpose for him. The dynamic linkages were at work.

His healthy security (in God, others, and himself), along with his more complete and positive identity, equipped him to better meet his need for belonging. Because he was more comfortable with himself, others were noticeably more comfortable with him. Also, because he knew himself better, he was able to determine whom he would enjoy as friends and who would enjoy relating to him. I'm glad he chose me!

After working at the seminary for two years, he attended my training course on learning styles. This helped him further understand how God designed him. I still remember the joy I experienced as I watched Dominick react to the content. I could almost see lightbulbs going on in his mind as he realized truths about himself. And I can still almost hear the enthusiasm with which he expressed his newfound joy and confidence. Understanding that he processed information differently than the majority of people led to his deeper acceptance of himself. He became more at ease in relating to others, even when the relationships were challenging. This new awareness helped him interpret a statement a university professor had made about him almost twenty-five years earlier: "This student has a sophisticated mind." (Without labeling the met needs in this paragraph, did you see still their positions and links as Dominick's view of his competence changed?)

Finally, after years of questioning his identity and why God made him the way He did, Dominick was able to say, "God created me this way on purpose and it's right!" This realization positively affected the four other needs. Within security, it was mainly his ability to be secure in himself that became healthier. It enhanced relationships, and his sense of belonging to God was richer as Dominick stopped asking, "Why do I think the way I do?" Dominick's purposes were clarified from the feedback he received, the input he was able to give others, and the joy he experienced in serving others. He always knew he was created to glorify God, but now he also believed God had given him a specific set of talents and gifts through which to do that. He no longer minded being different. He learned to appreciate his off-the-wall creative thinking and used it to benefit himself and others. His willingness to self-evaluate and rely on God, who gave him his abilities, led to feelings of competence in his character, attitudes, actions, and interactions.

Now, instead of having only a few needs met, Dominick has wholeness that is authentic.

I'm pleased to report that Dominick continues to analyze his feelings and actions in light of the five needs of the Model of Authentic Hope and Wholeness. He told me that hearing the seminar on the Model many years ago was another turning point for him, as was working on book projects with Lillian. The Model's interlocking, interactive components gave him a dynamic framework in which to put pieces of his life, see progress he had made, and comprehend why he had certain feelings. I'm grateful!

That's the beginning of Dominick's story. We'll return to his story, and Emily's, later.

PROBLEM-SOLVING POWER

Are you finding the Model of Authentic Hope and Wholeness helpful in illuminating both personal struggles and practical strategies for change in your life? I've taught this Model's principles to thousands of men, women, teenagers, and children on four continents, so far. If there is one dominant theme in the feedback I receive from people who apply its principles, it's that the Model serves as a practical problem-solving tool. Its life-changing principles hold true, whether people are followers of Jesus Christ or not, regardless of their age, gender, race, or country of origin. Praise God! I believe the Model ultimately works because the principles are based on biblical truth.

This section is about the Model's power for solving personal problems. I'll start by using the analogy of the Model's problem-solving sequence being like a ladder, with security (need #1) as the ground level, identity (#2) as the first rung up, belonging (#3) as the next rung up, followed by purpose (#4), with competence (#5) as the top rung. Here's the general four-step process I teach to resolve a problem, and after that, some specific examples that illustrate the principles. (I'll deal with some variations and additional details later.)

A. Identify the Problem and Unfulfilled Need

In other words, *What's my struggle? What deficiency have I noticed? In which component does it reside?* For example, no friends—belonging. Apathy—purpose. Too aggressive—security. (Don't worry if you're not sure you would have assigned these struggles to the components I did. You're just beginning to use this Model!)

B. Note the Sandwich of Needs

A sort of "sandwich" is created by the individual components directly below and directly above the "need at risk" that you identify. For instance, let's say my problem is in purpose (#4). It's sandwiched between belonging (#3) below and competence (#5) above.

C. Apply Practical Life Skills and Solutions to the Sandwich

Chapters 3, 4, and 6–8 provide detailed, practical, and relevant examples of how the five core needs can be fulfilled. Through explanations and illustrations, you'll learn how to determine if a need is being met in healthy ways, how to better meet that need, and how to then maintain wholeness. Each of those chapters includes details for a key "life skill" for the related core need. For instance, the life skill for identity (#2) is the change process, and the life skill for competence (#5) is decision making. These life skills won't repair all damage, so I've included other insights and instructions.

It's usually best to try to shore up the sandwich components before dealing directly with the at-risk need itself. Sometimes we'll know to repair something in the above need (for instance, working on competence to improve purpose). But it's usually more common to find that the lower sandwich component needs to be built up first (like working on belonging to increase or improve purpose). Remember the ladder analogy? A missing or broken lower rung can make it difficult or impossible to get where we want to go.

On the following page is a ladder chart of the five core needs and their related life skills, with security (#1) as the base.

THE LADDER OF CORE NEEDS AND LIFE SKILLS

NEED NO.	CORE NEED	LIFE QUESTION	LIFE SKILL
#5	Competence	*What do I do well?*	How to Make Decisions
#4	Purpose	*Why am I alive?*	How to Love God and Others
#3	Belonging	*Who wants me?*	How to Choose/Make/ Keep Friends
#2	Identity	*Who am I?*	How to Change
#1	Security	*Who can I trust?*	How to Forgive

D. Evaluate and Predict

A mind and heart quickened to evaluation serves us well as we apply this problem-solving strategy to our own struggles and those of others. This isn't about proving we're right—it's about helping ourselves and others mature. Therefore, I've learned to abandon midstream my assumption that a particular component was *the* culprit or that a life skill or other solution would definitely make a positive difference. For some people, issues are so complicated and deeply embedded that every need is met in unhealthy ways. Some trial-by-error attempts may, therefore, be necessary before finding ideas that resonate with those we're helping or with ourselves. But as we gain experience in thinking through the grid of the Model of Authentic Hope and Wholeness, our ideas will more often be on target. If we keep mindful of the future, it will prevent us from losing momentum and make continued progress more likely.

- First, this process works to improve the health of individual components and, as a result, helps people change from unhealthy or negative wholeness to healthy or positive wholeness.
- Second, establishing healthy wholeness is not the same as establishing authentic wholeness; where our ladder is grounded makes all the difference. If security is established on the ground with God through Christ, there is authentic hope and the potential for authentic wholeness if all five core needs are met through Him. Otherwise, the best that can be achieved is healthy wholeness. This is good, but it's not authentic wholeness.
- Third, it is possible to know and use all five life skills and other healthy behaviors and still be living in an unhealthy or inauthentic wholeness. For instance, how many people (Christians and non-Christians) do you know who are great at making friends—a part of the belonging life skill—but then use those friendships in order to manipulate people and get what they want from them? Is this healthy or authentic? I don't think so!

NONSANDWICH-RULE PROBLEM SOLVING

Let's look at an illustration that does not follow the sandwich rule. In this particular case, the practical solutions were found on the same rung as the felt need. It comes from my "too tall" slice-of-life illustration from chapter 1.

I told my mom I didn't want to be tall and clumsy anymore. It was my lack of belonging (#3), feeling too tall and not fitting in with my peers, that my parents identified as the problem. They arranged for me to have dance lessons. As a result, I became a tall dancer who wasn't clumsy and who was wanted by the other dancers. I liked being in the center of the dance line.

In this situation, the solution was found first in my at-risk need of belonging (#3), rather than in the sandwich components of identity (#2) and/or purpose (#4). My "problem" of being too tall and clumsy also put my identity at risk, since I had perceived an unchangeable characteristic (my height) as something negative. I was embarrassed by my height and occasional stumbles. But my felt need was belonging. That's what my parents addressed by signing me up for dance class.

Does it make sense that changing my belongingness changed my identity (#2)? That wasn't all. As I showed you in chapter 1, becoming a tap dancer positively met all five of my needs.

Betsy: Problem-Solving Solutions Applied to Life

Here's a more in-depth example of using this model for problem solving. The following illustrates steps in the process, which helped my niece Betsy:

Step A: Identify the Problem and Unfulfilled Need

My brother, Dave, married Debbie, one of my best friends. My love for them and their three precious children runs strong and deep. Praying for them is one of my greatest joys. A few years ago, I received more requests than usual asking me to pray for Betsy. Their fifteen-year-old ninth grader wasn't acting like her typical pleasant and obedient self. Her parents couldn't count on her to make wise choices. Dave and Debbie were rightly concerned. So was I.

What were her struggles? Which component were they most related to? What need didn't feel met? Betsy's identity (Who am I?) had collapsed for some reason.

Step B: Note the Sandwich of Needs

The effect each of the other needs has on identity is powerful and dynamic. When I begin problem solving, no matter which component I'm concerned about, I begin with the needs that surround it—in this case, security and belonging. Then, as appropriate, I go beyond the sandwich to include the other two needs.

Betsy's change in demeanor and character corresponded to two major events. First, she enrolled in a new school that was quite different from the one she had been attending. This sig-

nificantly influenced who she spent time with and who influenced her. What component does that have to do with? Right—belonging, the core need above her at-risk identity. Unfortunately, a student very unlike Betsy latched on to her. This one relationship chipped away at Betsy's moral and God-honoring behavior, which was a subset of her identity.

The change of schools also negatively influenced Betsy's security. (Did you already think of that? If you did, great!) She lost substantial relationships that answered the question, Who can I trust? *Teachers and peers she had counted on were no longer there for her. Neither was the routine of the previous school, along with its positive, trusting environment.*

Not long after Betsy's change in schools, a second event affected her security. Her dad decided to look for a new job, and he settled on an outstanding position that necessitated the family relocating to another state. No one was thrilled about having to move far away from their extended family and longtime friends. But the move was inevitable and the family knew it. My brother had already been working there and flying home about twice a month. At the time, there was substantial evidence God was orchestrating the move. That increased Debbie and Dave's optimism but didn't help Betsy in any obvious way.

What about you? When you were growing up, did you experience a major change in your family or community situation? Did it affect you in a different way than it did your siblings or peers? Not everyone responds the same to similar circumstances. That's one reason this book is not designed as a formula fix it. Andy, my nephew, and Katie, my other niece, weren't negatively affected in any noticeable ways by the change of schools, the impending move, or their dad's absence. Same family, same life events, different outcomes. Betsy's reactions to these changed situations led to unhealthy solutions to her needs.

Step C: Apply Practical Life Skills and Other Solutions

In this particular situation, there were several people who needed to apply practical solutions. I remain extremely proud of the way my brother and sister-in-law loved Betsy unconditionally through these valley experiences. They also responded decisively and with a very united front, even though my brother was regularly hundreds of miles away. And on top of that, they didn't ignore Katie or Andy either!

Dave and Debbie may not have consciously known to address Betsy's shaky identity by shoring up her security, but they figured out some specific and practical things to do that had exactly that effect. I'm sure these came to them in part as answers to prayers.

They instituted appropriate discipline, established a regular routine for her, and took away some of the freedoms she had earned earlier. Structure provides a type of security. Therefore, the structures that Dave and Debbie imposed on Betsy as a consequence for her foolish choices and actions actually enhanced her security.

Punishment or consequences may not always be enough to induce change. Neither is having right living modeled before us, even though I believe all three are significant. (Indeed, people will run from hypocrisy!)

To climb our wholeness ladders and avoid the chutes of life, we require learning and instruction that is optimistic and direct. We also need to be evaluated with honest and specific comments. Combined, these things help us know what to change and how to change.

Betsy benefited from her parents' practical instruction and feedback about choosing friends and how to appropriately end toxic friendships. Because she had to earn back her parents' trust, I know they had numerous conversations about accountability, responsibility, and behaving in trustworthy ways. My brother did his best to communicate with Betsy on a more regular basis, so she knew he was aware and involved in her life even though he wasn't always physically present. These conversations and changes improved her security.

After the move, Dave and Debbie purchased a home that's ideal for hosting parties, which perfectly fits with their gift of hospitality. This allowed them to be involved with their children and their children's friends (belonging). Dave and Debbie provided what practical changes they could as parents. But that would never have been enough to guarantee change. Betsy would have to make that choice.

In Betsy's case, she didn't need new life skills as much as she needed to change her attitudes toward her circumstances. That's what I mean by other solutions. *Sometimes strategies and skills—e.g., why and how to forgive and how to serve others—need to be taught, practiced, and even critiqued. At other times, adults can intervene and cause enough changes to remedy a situation and better meet a child's need. And in still other cases, God intervenes! Actually, I think a combination of all of the above is most common. Betsy used the skills she knew after making her decision to change.*

How did Betsy respond? When the family relocated to where Dave's new job was, Debbie and Dave enrolled Betsy in a school that was somewhere in between her two other school experiences. This new school felt safe to her, and it allowed her to grow. She didn't return to a pattern of poor choices. Instead, Betsy willingly made friends with some of the best kids in the school. This included a particular young man who was drawn to Betsy. "She's strong," he responded to my question about what he saw in her. "She knows what she's looking for, and she'll be sure to get there."

As I write this, Betsy has dated this same young man for over two years. Her boyfriend is a very positive influence on her, and he acknowledges that she's good for him too. Through this relationship, Betsy established herself in a church youth group with a good balance of fun activities and learning about God.

There's one more VIP whose responses I haven't mentioned yet. His interventions made all the difference for Dave, Debbie, and Betsy. As you've read these accounts, have you seen His hand in what happened?

I could have mentioned the absolutely strategic role God played at nearly every step in this family's story. I didn't do it so you'd have an opportunity to perhaps perceive His workings for yourself. Before I list some of how we saw God involved, perhaps you'd like to think of what you noticed.

God provided:
- the new job, which took Betsy away from a very unhealthy situation.
- the new school, where Betsy met peers and teachers who were a positive influence.
- the new house, where the family could entertain other teens and families.
- the strength Betsy needed to make the choice to change and follow through on all the smaller choices that followed.
- Dave and Debbie with unconditional love, strong support, and practical wisdom.

Dave and Debbie placed their security in God through Christ and the truth of Scripture. They were willing to be led by God's Spirit. I praise God they didn't wait until this difficult time to dig into the Word and listen to God. They were doing that all along. Let's not wait until the most desperate hours to be in the Word! Let's give it priority in our lives now!

After just three months of living where Betsy didn't originally want to, she said on Thanksgiving Day, "I'm grateful God can make good things out of bad situations." I believe the prayer and fasting that took place on Betsy's behalf was instrumental to her choosing obedience.

One more thing before we look at the next step. If Betsy's parents weren't as aware of her struggles, they wouldn't have provided her with the support structure she needed. Nor would they have made some of the strategic decisions they made when they moved across the country. It's always, always, always smart to be aware and to pray through and process ideas. Expect God to lead and answer!

Step D: Evaluate and Predict

You might approach this step differently than I do, and that's fine. The point is to be aware of what's working and what's not so you're prepared to shift directions, back up, or speed up, based on the evidence. For me, the "Evaluate and Predict" step is fulfilled by constantly asking questions. I might actually ask them during conversations with those involved. Often they simply guide my observations. The questions keep me alert to future possibilities, since being active rather than passive is essential.

In Betsy's case, I might have asked questions like these:

- Is there any evidence Betsy is still susceptible to negative peers? If so, how is she handling it? Is she allowing her character to be influenced positively or negatively?
- Is Betsy a positive influence on others? What's her motivation?
- How does Betsy currently describe herself (identity)?
- If Betsy's security weakens, how does she respond? What or who does she rely on in these times?
- How trustworthy has she become? Can her word be trusted?
- How aware is she of her parents' willingness to do just about anything to support her?
- What did Betsy learn about God from her chute and ladder experiences? What's the evidence?
- Did Andy and Katie learn anything valuable about God, their parents, Betsy, and/or themselves during these months? What's the evidence?
- Do Deb and Dave's commitments remain strong? Are they still united for their children? Still praying on their behalf?
- What did Debbie and Dave learn about God, Betsy, Katie, Andy, and/or themselves during these months? What's the evidence?

BUILDING
—ON—
THE ROCK

Maybe you'll be putting this book down soon to rest or take care of some of your many responsibilities. May I ask you to first spend a few minutes with the following authenticity checkpoints? I believe this section of reflection will be good use of your time. I've designed it to be a tool for you to make the components of the Model practical in your life.

> *Based on what you've read, think of two or more things you're grateful for understanding.*
> *What are some ways that at least one of your five core needs has been met?*
> *If you know God personally, through His Son Jesus Christ, remind yourself of ways He has already fulfilled these various needs in your life and ask His Spirit to continue His work in you as it relates to these five core needs.*
> *What questions do you have that you hope I answer in later chapters?*
> *For hope and wholeness to be authentic, we need to anchor our thoughts and actions on God's Word. As a practical exercise, locate the following Scriptures. You may want to write them out on index cards or recite them aloud. For some of us, the act of writing will help anchor the truths in our minds, for others seeing them does that, and for others hearing the verses aloud is meaningful. Lamentations 3:25; Colossians 1:27; 1 John 1:9; Deuteronomy 31:6; Ephesians 2:10; Philippians 4:19; Hebrews 6:19; and Isaiah 26:4.*

We have this hope [Jesus] as an anchor for the soul, firm and secure.

—Hebrews 6:19

Christ is all, and is in all.

—Colossians 3:11

THREE

SECURITY
Who Can I Trust?

THIS EVENING AS I WRITE this chapter, an incident with a lost boy in a grocery store reminded me that when a major source of security is no longer present or working in our lives, nothing else matters.

What about you? Who is your security? Who do you trust? Or have you placed your security in things, rather than trustworthy people? Establishing and maintaining security is vital. Without it, healthy identity, belonging, purpose, and competence are not possible.

Attempting to fulfill our security need through things is common, and dangerous. No answer to the question "*What* can I trust?" provides lasting security. Things fade away, break down, and lose their glamour. Disappointment follows and despair may be on its heels.

Still, many children and adults try to base their security on things like popularity, grades, income, knowledge, talent, and being "cool." When these fade, it shatters their worlds. For example, children who base their security on "being cool" can die on the inside anytime they don't believe they are perceived as being cool by enough people or by the right people. Then they can get desperate—either trying to reestablish coolness as their security, or trying something else as their anchor.

Until they reach a point of trusting in people instead of things, they'll be at risk for not having any of their needs met. (Does that make sense in light of this Model's dynamic sequence?)

I believe there are three sources that are able to provide solid security: (1) God, (2) trustworthy people, and (3) ourselves—and in that order. Our security is strongest and healthiest when we put our trust in all three, in appropriate ways. We'll spend the rest of this chapter exploring what that means and how it is achieved. I've included some slice-of-life stories and suggested ways you can reflect on the sources of security in your own life.

SOURCE ONE: GOD SECURITY

Our deepest need for security is met through a personal relationship with God. By anchoring ourselves and our lives to Jesus Christ, we can be confident that our security is rock solid. In Jesus Christ, our future is secure. He's our Savior and Deliverer. In the present, we can rely daily upon our Father's love, the leading of His Holy Spirit, and Jesus to be our Lord.

Our faith, which is our vital connection to this trustworthy Trinity, sustains us whenever we find ourselves in situations that seem like hell on earth. We need to turn to God, rely on Him, and trust Him at all times—even when life doesn't make sense or we feel like God doesn't care.

Especially in the midst of our emotional earthquakes, we need to open His Word to be taught or reminded that God truly is dependable.[1] He is on our side and never against us—even though He allows hard things to happen.

The Bible clearly shows us that we are not His robots or marionette puppets that He controls. (God loves us enough to even give us the power and responsibility of choosing Him, rather than forcing us to yield ourselves to Him.) Neither does God always overrule the unwise, evil, or stupid choices that all of us make at times as broken, sinful people. Yet when we recognize sin as sin and confess it, God's Word tells us that because of Jesus' sacrifice, He forgives us completely and cleanses away the guilt, while loving us unconditionally through it all. There's tremendous freedom in embracing the truth that there's nothing we can do to cause God to love us any more or any less!

These things are true, whether or not we've personally experienced them, and whether or not we feel them. When Scripture teaches us something, we need to go with truth instead of our feelings. It may not always be easy. But we find a perfect source of security in God through Christ.

. . . .

BUILDING
—ON—
THE ROCK

Some opposites of security are anxiety, fear, and doubt. If our security isn't established in God, we may flounder around like a fish out of water. These and other negative responses to our circumstances and interactions may affect our spiritual growth.

I've found comfort from Psalm 46. We're taught in the first verse that "God is our refuge and strength, an ever-present help in trouble." After references to natural disasters and wars in verses 2–9, we read verse 10: "Be still, and know that I am God." I'm so encouraged by this instruction! No matter what's going on in our personal lives or the world, God asks us to remember that He is God and we can be still. When we know who God is and what He does, we can more easily quiet our minds and hearts, stop wondering and worrying, and just *be.*

How much security do you currently place in God? If you're not sure, think about your thoughts and behaviors over the past few days. Our trust in God shows up in our walk and our talk. Have you experienced significant levels of anxiety, fear, doubt, and/or questions about God's ability or availability?

> ▸ *If God has been a steady source of security for you, perhaps you could spend some time praying about or*

writing down the blessings for which you are thankful. If art is a better medium than writing for you, create something that reminds you of God's trustworthiness. Or compose a poem or song.

▸ If you want God to reveal more of His trustworthiness to you, ask Him to do just that. He can do it for others in your life, too, so I encourage you to also pray for them.

▸ Go on daily "God hunts," as my friend Bethany calls them. Let me pass on her challenge: Open your spiritual eyes to see God daily and your ears to hear from Him. Rather than believing in luck or coincidences, recognize God's role in what is happening around you, for you, and in you. (Remember my friend Emily from chapter 1? She doesn't believe in coincidences anymore. Instead we talk about "Godcidents.")

▸ You and/or your family could begin a study of God's names. This can be an ideal way to strengthen your security in Him.

▸ You may benefit from joining a small group to search Scriptures. Many people find the interaction stimulating and rewarding.

▸ We've posted information about choosing Jesus as your personal Lord and Savior on our Web site. Just click on the link for chapter 3 at www.AuthenticHope.com. Establishing your security in God through a relationship with Jesus Christ is the most important thing you can ever do!

. . . .

SOURCE TWO: OTHERS SECURITY

Let's analyze how we develop security in others by investigating first what prevents it. For one thing, sins get in the way, don't they? In any relationship, whenever someone makes choices that violate trust or inject the DNA of doubt, everyone involved pays a severe price. That's true, whether that person is a spouse, child, parent, roommate, coworker, or friend. Not being trusted—having our word questioned, our e-mail monitored, and our motives doubted—is not a pleasant consequence of sin. It's deserved though. Without security and trust, relationships won't flourish. Actually that's an understatement. I believe that without trust, relationships won't last. The strain becomes too difficult.

Are deceit and lies the only trust violators? They may be the most obvious, but many choices and behaviors can subtly shake our security as relationships change from healthy to unhealthy. Unless we decide to do repair work that reestablishes security, broken relationships die.

Building and Rebuilding Trust

My friends and I have built some solid relationships over the years. Sadly, not all stay strong. Sometimes broken friendships have been repaired successfully, and for that, I'm grateful. At other times, even with intentional change and effort on my part or theirs, restoration hasn't been possible. Sometimes my friends and I don't try to reconstruct relationships. Therefore, we don't regain what we had (or what we thought we had). Our history, the extent of our trust at the time of its violation, and my sense of the other person's motives help me decide if they're safe or unsafe, trustworthy or untrustworthy. "Why did she do what she did? Why was that decision made? Did she really have my best interests at heart?" In the sad cases, I grieve the death of the relationship and choose to move forward and invest my energies elsewhere.

In chapter 6, we'll explore the life skill of friendship and principles for building healthy security in others. In the rest of this section, I'd like to share illustrations and principles that can be used when rebuilding broken relationships is appropriate.

Miles, Maria, and Jazzy

Some people never recover from the loss of security caused by divorce and lose out on meaningful relationships because of their inability to trust again. Others do quite well as they work through disappointment and pain. That is what Miles has done. I am reminded of

Scriptures that teach that growth occurs during suffering (e.g., Romans 5:3; James 1:2–4).

Miles is one of my heroes when it comes to growing through a time of shattered security. Unfortunately, he and his wife, Maria, divorced a year ago. Miles showed maturity by dealing with some of his problems instead of ignoring his sins, weaknesses, and unhealthy thought patterns. He chose to examine himself, respond appropriately to the Holy Spirit's leading, and not blame Maria for all their marriage difficulties. Miles also sought out and responded to godly counsel and has been even more involved in worship and learning. Miles ran toward God—rather than running from Him, an all-too-common reaction to traumatic breaks in relational trust.

When Miles became acutely aware of his failings, he didn't think first and foremost about how they had affected Maria. His primary concern was how his choices and interaction patterns grieved God. (I think that's the right order of concerns, even though thinking about how we hurt others can also lead us to consider how we grieved God.) Miles will tell you, with a smiling face, that he's a better person now than three years ago when he and Maria first separated. And he'll give God all the credit. His transparency humbles and inspires me!

Miles still wears his wedding ring. He prays faithfully for God to restore his marriage. I won't be shocked if that's exactly what God does. But that possibility isn't what has motivated Miles's growth. Changing in God-honoring ways, and not merely Maria-honoring ways, is his goal.

I visited Miles a few days ago. He said when praying for their four-year-old daughter, Jazzy, recently, he sensed God leading him to ask something he never had before. As a man learning obedience, Miles didn't hesitate to ask, "God, please give me favor with Jazzy." The next time he picked her up at Maria's, he sensed Jazzy relating to him differently.

"Kathy," he said smiling, "she softened toward me." He held his hand to his heart, and continued, "I believe her fear and doubt are gone." We're praising God for demonstrating His love and compassion by suggesting the prayer and answering it. He does heal the brokenhearted (Psalm 147:3), including Jazzy.

On the one-year anniversary of his divorce, Miles heard God suggest this same prayer, but this time for his ex-wife, Maria. So he obeyed and prayed for favor with her and believes God will strengthen their bond, if for no other reason than to increase Jazzy's security.

Forgiveness, forgiveness, forgiveness. Are you surprised I haven't mentioned it or are you surprised that I am now? I believe it's the foundation of ongoing security in others. Miles and Maria needed to forgive each other in order to move on by healing, growing individually, and relating together. As they have, Jazzy's security is strengthened, and therefore, so are possibilities for healthier identity, belonging, purpose, and competence.

Who else needed to be forgiven in this situation? Miles needed to forgive himself and Maria needed to forgive herself. Right? I don't know about you, but for me, this can be more challenging than forgiving those who hurt me. We'll come back to the subject of forgiveness as this chapter closes, so keep processing any thoughts you have and keep the topic in mind as you keep reading.

Christlike Friends

We all need to choose to invest in relationships with people whose love is like God's: consistent, unconditional, merciful, and personal. Christlike people will prove themselves trustworthy more often than other people do. They will positively affect our security, just as Miles is having a healthier impact in the lives of Jazzy and Maria. (However, people demonstrating God's type of love can still disappoint us at times. I've found, though, that when Christlike friends let us down, it's rarely intentional, and we seldom suffer huge wounds that don't heal.)

Who demonstrates consistent and unconditional love for you— in good times and bad, and whether they need something from you or not? These people may voice disapproval at times. From them, it doesn't indicate a loss of love. The exact opposite is often true. Their willingness to risk rejection is further evidence of the depth of their love.

Who shows gracious love to you—love that is compassionate when you haven't done anything to deserve it? In fact, we may have behaved in such a way that makes it easy for people to abandon us and stop loving us. When they don't, that's merciful love.

Personal love is such a gift, isn't it? Christlike friends get to know us intimately and show their love for us in personal, meaningful ways. If we enjoy sunsets, our friends will watch with us. They'll play a certain song for us when they know it will soothe us. When they know we're lonely, they'll call or stop by. Who cares enough about you to love you personally—in ways that indicate your likes, dislikes, concerns, and passions are taken into consideration?

. . . .

BUILDING
—ON—
THE ROCK

As an introvert who is very comfortable being alone, I sometimes joke about how hard it was for me to open up to people—not only for godly counsel but for fun as well. It was prideful of me to think I didn't need anybody. I'm a better person today because I've chosen to build relationships with trustworthy people who understand me. I have more fun too!

I'm also more secure in others. Two years after moving to Fort Worth, Texas, to begin the ministry of Celebrate Kids, Inc., I purchased a home. Zach's help made it possible. He walked through the house with me and determined it was in excellent condition and being offered at a fair price. You see, Zach is a friend from church who builds homes for a living. I knew I could trust him to look for assets and problems differently than I could. I still remember the heightened sense of relief I experienced when Zach suggested I buy the house.

What about you? How secure are you with key people in your life? Who has blessed you with trustworthy input? Have you thanked them? Would it prove beneficial to ask a friend for a rating on your trustworthiness? What about sharing with another why you give him or her a certain rating?

Are any relationships suffering hidden structural damage because of violations of security? Maybe now is the time to talk about design flaws and make some new blueprints.

. . . .

SOURCE THREE: SELF-SECURITY

As important as it is to find our foundational security in God, and to have a select group of trustworthy people in our lives, we also have a deep-down need to trust ourselves. Do you agree, or does that thought alarm you—or perhaps both?

You might be familiar with Proverbs 3:5, which teaches, "trust in the LORD with all your heart and lean not on your own understanding." It's absolutely true! However, I don't believe my recommendation to learn to trust ourselves contradicts this Scripture. I'm not suggesting we trust in what we know or what we can do rather than in God. That would be foolish. Trusting God is always essential, even when we think we understand something completely or know we can do something well.

We shouldn't attempt to meet our need for self-security through our competence (what we do or how well we do it). If we do, then when we don't meet our own or someone else's definition of excellence, the emptiness can consume us. We may look alive on the outside but be dead on the inside. Another chunk of ourselves chips off of whatever wholeness we had, hope vanishes, and despair sets in.

So, if by saying we need to be able to trust ourselves I *don't* mean that we shouldn't trust God, and I *don't* mean that we should place our security in what we do, what exactly *do* I mean?

Meeting our need for self-security *does* happen when we consistently do the right things right, in every area of life, even when no one is watching or aware. Righteousness, not competence, is the big test. In both our being and our doing, right is right. Developing righteousness requires a lot of self-examination:

- Will I be patient when the car in front of me is going much slower than I prefer?
- Will I eat healthy food, even when I think I can "sneak" the unhealthy stuff by?
- Will I be joyful during trying circumstances?
- Will I exaggerate so my story is more exciting, or will I tell the truth?
- Will I take appropriate responsibility for my part in a conflict?
- Will I do what I've told others I will do (e.g., finishing a work-related report by the next morning or returning phone calls)?
- Am I willing to be unpopular for a while for the sake of righteousness?
- Can I trust myself to make right decisions and to solve personal and relational problems wisely?

Here's a personal example of how I'm exercising discipline because I want to do the right things right. I travel a lot, so I eat many meals in restaurants. Maturing in my weight control is an area where I need more self-security. Especially within the past eight months, my resolve to be more consistent has intensified, so I've instituted certain behaviors. For example, when I'm concerned I'll have less self-control than I need, I don't even open the restaurant's menu. I'm sunk if I see pictures of juicy steaks, loaded baked potatoes, and onion rings on the side! Perhaps you can relate. I simply ask my server to describe their salads. They're willing to do this, even though they tell me where they're listed in the menu in my hand. This one simple decision has helped.

Self-security is dependent upon our desire to live righteously, be obedient, and be self-disciplined. It isn't about perfection. It's about being the people we were created to be and doing what it takes to get there. It's about gaining greater consistency in making wise choices (including whom we choose to trust). It's about integrity in choosing to rely on God's empowerment for change, sinning less than we used to, and developing more maturity. And this makes us more self-trusting as well as more trustworthy for others!

BUILDING
—ON—
THE ROCK

What about you? Can you trust yourself to do the right things right? Maybe you could choose an area of self-security to examine and improve. Do you keep your word? Are you on time? Do you respond angrily again after resolving to be more compassionate?

Do certain things seem to trigger these negative behaviors? If so, how could their occurrence be decreased? How will you know when you've made progress? Do you need to tell someone about this process and what you're experiencing, or are you content just to know for yourself?

Our self-security definitely influences how much others trust us. If you set a goal to develop more trusting relationships, you may want to set a prerequisite goal for personal trustworthiness. Progress here will show up there. Our self-security increases when we humbly and courageously identify areas of untrustworthiness within ourselves. From the self-evaluation we do, with God's guidance and empowerment, we can set specific goals and choose action steps to accomplish them.

But what happens when we fail in that process? Or when others fail us? Then the life skill of forgiveness comes into play.

LIFE SKILL: FORGIVENESS

Security is founded on forgiveness. Those who believe in Jesus Christ for their salvation can be secure in God knowing He forgives us when we sin (Ephesians 1:7; Colossians 1:13–14; 1 John 1:9). We don't have to prove ourselves, promise we'll do this or that, or punish ourselves. We just have to ask Him to lift the weight of our sin and entrust Him to do it since Jesus' death paid the penalty that our sins deserve.

If we want relationships to stay healthy, it's absolutely necessary to forgive those who sin against us or who simply disappoint us for any number of reasons. Forgiving others and ourselves is critical for us if we want to attain and maintain emotional and spiritual health.

Here are some practical things I've learned about the process of forgiveness:[2]

- I just need to do it! Obedience is always right and Scripture teaches us to forgive. When obedience isn't enough of a motive, I remember that if I don't forgive those who sin against me, I'm not forgiven by God (Matthew 6:14–15). At the same time, I remember how much Jesus forgave me and that forgiveness is possible only in God's strength, with His love.
- If I'm struggling to forgive myself, it's almost always related to pride. I have to acknowledge I'm not perfect—I'm always capable of mistakes and inflicting pain. I also must be willing to put others first. To forgive, I must meditate upon the truth that God honors the humble (e.g., Psalm 51:17; Proverbs 18:12; Matthew 23:12).
- A prayer in which I ask God to forgive me is essential. I can't just think it in my head or talk about it with others, even though that usually helps me identify the specifics. I must enter into God's presence, letting Him know directly that I'm aware of my sin and I'm sorry for it. A humble and detailed prayer honors Him and indicates more trust. Although He hears "flare prayers" like, "Oh, God, forgive me!" that we shout on the way out the door, I believe a depth of healing accompanies more specific prayers.
- After confessing my sins to God, I shouldn't wonder if I've been forgiven. I have been, because that's what His Word teaches (Ephesians 1:7; 1 John 1:9). I may not instantly *feel* better or any closer to God—that's one of the consequences of sin. But I choose to believe I'm forgiven. If the sin or the relationship continues to be on my mind or if a sense of distance from God lasts, it often signals other sins I wasn't aware of. For example, I might have asked to be forgiven of my pessimism, but not the accompanying lack of faith. I've looked forward to the times of refreshment that follow forgiveness (Acts 3:19).

- Even if I don't understand why people are hurt by what I've done, I need to ask God to forgive me and apologize to those I've hurt and also ask for their forgiveness. Because these prayers to God and apologies to others can be somewhat vague, this may come across as a contradiction to the previous statement, but it's not. Of course, when I know more specifics, it does me a world of good to acknowledge them. Yet even when I don't understand the details, but I have a general knowledge of the wrong, that's no excuse for not seeking forgiveness. Also, when I hear myself say, "I'm sorry *if* I hurt you," instead of "I'm sorry *that* I hurt you," I want to just kick myself. This is such a slam and a cop-out. Saying *if* implies I'm not taking responsibility for my actions and invalidates their impact on the other person.
- I don't necessarily need to tell others when I forgive them. Sometimes they don't even know they hurt me. That's often okay. Whether I let them know or not depends upon the depth of our relationship, plus any specific guidance received from the Holy Spirit.
- I don't need to know when others forgive me. It's nice to know, but not essential. And whether they have or haven't shouldn't influence my behavior toward them.
- Everyone benefits when I name my sins. Would you agree that it's much easier to pray, "God, forgive me for sinning against my dad," than it is to pray, "God, forgive me for disrespecting my dad by not completely listening to his question before I jumped in with my answer"? Naming the sin helps with closure. I believe it helps me sin less in the same way. And when talking with my dad, it shows him that I'm aware of and taking responsibility for the specifics.
- Forgiving and forgetting are not the same. Forgiving someone means I will not bring up the sin again. Therefore, in time, I will actually forget it. But it's more of a "not remembering" issue than a "forgetting" issue. I don't waste my energy trying to forget. Rather, I intentionally choose to not remember. When I'm frustrated because this isn't always easy, I celebrate the reality that God does both—He totally and unconditionally forgives His children, and He doesn't remember our sin (Hebrews 8:12; 10:17).
- When I struggle to put sin behind me, I read, reread, and read again chapter 6 of Romans.

Search me, O God, and know my heart;
test me and know my anxious thoughts.
See if there is any offensive way in me,
and lead me in the way everlasting.
–Psalm 139:23-24

. . . .

REVISITING
—THE—
DYNAMIC SEQUENCE

An inability to trust ourselves, others, and God is especially troublesome because of the effect it has on our other core needs. Deciding I can't trust myself makes me insecure and gives me a very negative identity. (*Who am I?* "I'm someone who can't be trusted.")

Identity controls behavior, so my negative identity can cause behaviors that may leave my need for belonging unmet. For example, if I now distance myself from people because I believe I can't be trusted, I'll have fewer chances to build a healthy network of belonging.

Without a solid belonging, I may not know whom to love and serve, so purpose is difficult to establish.

And without purpose, I have no reason to need competence. (I don't need to be good at anything if I have no reason to be alive.)

Competence loops back to security and starts another layer of transformation. When I recognize God as my source of competence and I've learned skills to strengthen my abilities, my security will be much stronger.

BUILDING
—ON—
THE ROCK

▸ *Based on what you read, think of two or more things you're grateful for understanding about security.*

▸ *Which sources of your security—God, others, or self— do you perceive as strongest right now? What can you do to maintain or further establish that status? Which source would you like to see significantly strengthened? What practical things does this chapter's section on this source suggest? What will you do? How could this involve others? When will you follow through?*

▸ *Think of two or more questions you hope I answer in the next chapter about identity or the link between security and identity.*

▸ *You might want to spend some time with recommended Scripture verses related to this chapter. You'll find some listed on our Web site. Click on the chapter 3 link at www.AuthenticHope.com.*

*Sovereign LORD, you have made the
heavens and the earth
by your great power and outstretched arm.
Nothing is too hard for you.*

—Jeremiah 32:17

FOUR

IDENTITY
Who Am I?

HER BRIGHT RED HAIR caused her to stand out at the conference in Southeast Asia. With the other children, she appeared to be concentrating on my "Authentic Hope" message. They were enthusiastic as we discussed truthful answers to the identity question: *Who am I?* Children described themselves as "creative, outgoing, good soccer players, Christians, Grandma's favorites," etc.

As I transitioned to instruction regarding possible negative answers to the same question, the quiet and calm that came over the children was a definite contrast to their earlier exuberance. After explaining that it's prideful to only know our positives, I asked them to think of one negative thing about themselves that could be changed, perhaps a sin that was making God unhappy. I then shared the great news from Ephesians 4:22–24 that change is possible when we know what's wrong, what's right, and we rely on the Holy Spirit as we make intentional efforts to change. I explained that transformation happens when we confront and reject wrong or unhealthy beliefs, feelings, behaviors, attitudes, or actions that we're holding on to.

Among the points I made were these: Change will most likely occur when we think of opposites of the negative. (For example, if we don't want to procrastinate anymore, we can think about becoming more timely, active, motivated, persevering, diligent, focused, considerate of others' schedules, and less concerned with perfection.) And change is more likely when we dig deeper to discover the reasons we behave the way we do. I demonstrated this thinking process with a few examples from my own life.

I wasn't sure how much the younger children understood until the next day. One set of parents took the time to tell me their daughter, Rachel, shared details from my entire talk with them. How encouraging! She especially stressed the idea that, with God's help, we can take off our old self and put on our new self. Then Rachel asked them to help her with the third step—changing her mind through purposeful study of God's Word. *Yes!*

Rachel told her parents that while I was teaching, she remembered earlier times when they had talked with her about interrupting. For her, one answer to the question, *Who am I?* was "I'm an interrupter."

So later that night, Rachel asked her mom and dad to help her find Bible verses about interrupting. She taught them what I had taught her—that she should read and study relevant Proverbs. She should also find passages showing that Jesus didn't interrupt when He could have. (Since verse 24 in Ephesians 4 asks us to become more like God, I recommend studying Jesus' character.) They also talked about why Rachel interrupted and what might help her stop. Needless to say, these parents were beaming as they shared this with me and I was encouraged too.

Two nights later, when the conference was over and people were saying their good-byes, this mom again approached me. We were enjoying our talk when, from the other end of the room, the girl with bright red hair came running in our direction. She began shouting, "Mommy! Mommy! Mommy!" as only happy little girls can. This is when I learned this mom's daughter was that especially attentive learner from Wednesday. Even when at her mom's elbow, Rachel continued, but with more time between each repetition and more of an edge and whine to her voice.

We both tried to ignore Rachel for a while, but it wasn't quieting her. So, her mom turned, made eye contact, and without expressing emotion stated, "You are interrupting."

I wish you could have seen the look of horror on Rachel's face! It was instantaneous. This was the very thing she told God she wouldn't do! She immediately clasped her hand over her mouth and became statuelike while her mother and I continued our conversation. When we finished, we both thanked "the statue" for waiting her turn. Then the mother willingly asked what was so important.

Rather than answering her mother's question, the first words out of the once-again-alive little girl were, "It worked Mommy! Just like we thought it would! I kept saying what I wanted to tell you and I still remember it . . ." She proceeded to fill her mom in as I moved on to say good-bye to others.

IDENTITY: WHO AM I?

Our identity—how we define and describe ourselves—controls our behavior. That's one reason identity is so important. For instance, a woman who thinks she is creative (her identity) may eagerly await a meeting with her supervisor who wants and needs new solutions for a long-standing problem. At the meeting, she won't hesitate to share what others might think are strange ideas if she thinks her supervisor will categorize them as "creative."

But what if someone doesn't think well of himself and answers the identity question of *Who am I?* negatively? For example, "I never think of workable ideas." He'll probably be stressed, both prior to a meeting and during it. This low expectation may further cement his negative identity since he probably won't share his ideas very much. Therefore, he may leave the meeting saying to himself: "See, I did it again. I'm not helping anybody!" And the supervisor might think, "I can't count on him to help solve problems."

What about Rachel? Because she developed a habit of interrupting, her parents believed it was important to bring it to her attention. Because Rachel was told she interrupted, her identity became, "I'm an interrupter." Because identity controls behavior, stopping her negative communication pattern actually became more difficult once Rachel applied this label to herself. That's why strategic planning and her parents' support were necessary for Rachel to make wise choices. If they now talk less about her interrupting and thank her when she doesn't do it, her identity will become, "I'm not an interrupter. I am patient." This will further establish her new behavior pattern of waiting her turn to talk. Identity and behavior go hand in hand.

We saw another example of behavior that influenced identity when I introduced you to Dominick in chapter 2. When Lillian positively evaluated Dominick's editing ability, his identity became, "I'm an effective editor." This gave him the confidence to write his own pieces. Therefore, he became a writer. But he didn't stop there. Because he defined himself as a writer, he eventually became a published author. He believed he had something to offer people—an indicator of belonging and purpose. Understanding the various learning styles helped him appreciate and accept his innate thinking abilities, and his identity shifted from the generic, "I can contribute," to the specific, "I can be a valuable and unique contributor to other people's projects."

Dominick's story demonstrates how one identity leads to another identity, which leads to another and another and another. This is often the way it is. Still, I meet many people who want a big change in their behaviors, but haven't thought about the necessary small changes and gradual shifts in identity required to become that person. It's rare (if not impossible!) to move directly from point A to point E without spending at least some time at points B, C, and D.

. . . .

BUILDING
—ON—
THE ROCK

What about you? What's your identity? (Or should I say, what are your identities?) How do you describe or define yourself? If someone said, "Tell me about yourself," what would you say?

Before I influence your thinking any further, I encourage you to complete the accompanying chart by writing down twenty statements that describe you. Don't worry yet about what the other columns are for.

. . . .

#	Identity Statements			
1				
2				
3				
4				
5				
6				
7				
8				
9				
10				
11				
12				
13				
14				
15				
16				
17				
18				
19				
20				

IS YOUR IDENTITY COMPLETE?

God has made us complex, so there are many ways we can define ourselves. For example, I use these eight identity categories: intellectual, emotional, social, character qualities, physical, career, material possessions, and spiritual.

Intellectual

I'm especially concerned when school-age children don't include anything about their intellectual selves when describing who they are (e.g., I'm quick at math, I enjoy scientific problem solving, I'm not good with details, history fascinates me, spelling is hard for me). But it's even right for adults to describe themselves in terms of intellectual attributes. Remember, identity and behavior go hand in hand. If we don't think of ourselves as smart, we may not exercise our mental abilities when appropriate. We may not volunteer for certain opportunities (e.g., writing for the church newsletter, making posters to advertise a community outreach, researching a quote's accuracy for our pastor) where we could have been a tremendous blessing. Did you list anything related to your intellectual self?

Emotional

Many people don't include the category of emotions when defining themselves. And I've found that most who do usually list difficult emotional states or feelings such as: I'm apathetic, I'm depressed, I'm confused, nothing makes sense to me, I'm sad a lot, I'm angry. Emotions themselves are not sin—though at times they may be the cause or result of sin.

Of course, change from destructive to constructive emotional responses isn't possible until we recognize our unhealthy emotions exist, and we perceive them as something we can and should change. Look back at your list. Did you include anything from this category?

Social

Age may influence how many social identity statements you included on your list. For example, teens and young adults will often include as many as ten to fifteen statements about their social selves. Some girls list things like the following: "I'm going out with Blake. I used to date Josiah. I don't want to have anything to do with Miguel." And boys may list: "No one likes me, but I like Jill and Hailey. I wish Cole and Sergio would be friends with me."

What about you? Did you list significant family relationships and/or friends? What order are they in? If you're married with children, I hope "wife/husband" is listed before "mother/father."

Are you surprised or alarmed by anything you did or did not list from this category?

Character Qualities

When making your list, did you include words that describe your character? You might have included attributes such as: dependable, self-disciplined, courageous, respectful, selfish, engaging, or rude. Although some character qualities can be assigned to other categories (e.g., rudeness could be part of our social identity), I prefer to emphasize our character by making it a separate category.

Including character qualities within your twenty statements is a sign of maturity, whether the identities you described are positive or negative. Character makes up the foundation of who we are. It influences all we do and every interaction we have. It's based in the heart, which is what God examines, so it's important to ask ourselves how we're doing in this area.

Physical: Abilities, Looks, Health

Physical identity is another category that can be influenced by age, with younger people usually including it more often than do older individuals. What about your list? Is the physical ability subcategory included (e.g., I play basketball with the neighborhood guys, I'm out of shape, I'm good with my hands)? Is the physical looks subcategory on your list (e.g., I have naturally curly hair. My complexion is great. I'm tall. I'm overweight. I hate my nose.)? And is the third subcategory of physical health represented (e.g., I have cancer. I am twenty pounds lighter. My arthritis is acting up.)?

Although statements describing our physical looks might be included on our identity lists at times, it's important to remember God's admonition. His holy Word, in 1 Samuel 16:7, sets the standard: "The LORD does not look at the things man looks at. Man looks at the outward appearance, but the LORD looks at the heart." I wonder if this is why people in the Bible are rarely described? I've noticed that descriptions are included when physical features are relevant. For example, we learn Esther is beautiful because she's being considered as the next queen of Persia. It's a relevant detail because the king would take physical appearance into account when making his decision.

Look back at your list of identity statements. Are the physical abilities, looks, and/or health subcategories over- or underemphasized?

Career

Perhaps you listed what you do to earn a living. Men often do and most admit it's high in their list of twenty statements. It can be for women too. (If you listed it before "husband/wife" and "father/mother," how about committing to change the order? Remember, identity controls behavior.) Those who prioritize their career when answering the question, *Who am I?* are the ones who may struggle most with the thought of retirement. And the possibility of losing a job can be especially terrifying to them. Did you include this category?

Material Possessions

Ideally, this category didn't even make our list. It sometimes does, though. For instance, I've met children who tell me they own seventy-two Beanie Babies and teens that tell me how many DVDs or CDs they have.

Sometimes we adults include things, too, and that says something about us. For example, if people define themselves by statements such as, "I have a bigger pool than anyone on my street," what can we immediately conclude about their security? I would suggest that people's identity always points to their security. This pool owner has placed at least a part of his or her security in things, income, and/or being the biggest and best. What about you?

Spiritual

Have you wondered when I'd get to this category? I hope you included it on your list. Actually, I hope it's mentioned among your top five statements. If you mentioned it at all, what did you include and how did you word it? God tells us who we are throughout the pages of His Word. Here are some of the many, many correct statements about our spiritual identities: All people are created in God's image, and Jesus died for all of us. Believers are saved and forgiven from their sins through faith in Christ, deeply and permanently loved and complete in Him. We should consider ourselves dead to sin and put on the full armor of God to survive spiritual warfare (Genesis 1:27; Romans 5:8; 6:11; 8:39; Ephesians 1:7; 2:8; 6:10–18; 2 Peter 1:3).[1]

IS YOUR IDENTITY ACCURATE?

Present vs. Past

Remember, the identity question is not, "Who *was* I?" Perhaps you remember from my illustration in chapter 1, that I was clumsy as a young girl. It's no longer on my list. If it was, I'd be more apt to trip and stumble. I transitioned from "clumsy" to "not as clumsy as I used to be" to "no longer clumsy" to not even thinking to list it when answering the *Who am I?* question.

We can sometimes fall back into a past identity when we are around people who don't know who we currently are. This can be why some adult children and their parents struggle. If it's been a long time since adult children moved out of their parents' home, and they only see each other once or twice a year, both parents and children may relate based on old identities. Ignoring the changes can make for challenging conversations. This same conflict can occur between grandparents and grandchildren who change dramatically between visits. Are your identities based on the present?

Present vs. Future

Not only is the identity question not, "Who *was* I?" it's also not, "Who do I *want* to be?" I'm all for people having goals to work toward, but there's danger in defining ourselves with too many future-oriented statements or unrealistic dreams. For example, I'd be concerned if someone began their list with, "I'll be happy in three months when we move." Sometimes that kind of sentiment leads to hopelessness, especially if people don't have the skills or support to get from where they are to where they want to be—or if the solution is out of their control. Did you list any identities that are future oriented or unrealistic?

Blind Spots

Another factor that can lead to an inaccurate identity is the existence of blind spots. When making your list of statements, did you exclude obvious strengths, weaknesses, and/or sin you're struggling with? Think about it this way: If people who know you well listed twenty true statements about you, how similar to your list would theirs be? What might it suggest if others list descriptors you don't, such as: insecure, angry, life of the party, deep thinker, or worrier?

Our preference, at moments like these, is probably to believe the good attributes but dismiss the challenging ones. (Granted, some people may accept the bad ones and minimize the good ones.) Prayer would be a mature response! We can ask God to reveal truths about our identity. Asking these friends for their input can be very revealing and humbling. If we decide they're right, and we do have, for instance, a tendency to be angry, then we need to determine why we are, what we can do about the root issues, and how we need to learn to respond instead. (We'll detail such aspects of the transformation process in the next chapter.)

DO YOU HAVE A POSITIVE IDENTITY?

This week, I've been on two radio talk shows targeted to parents of school-age children. I asked listeners to be more positive than negative when thinking about their children's teachers and interacting with them. I asked them to believe the best of these teachers, find something good they're doing, and thank and encourage them more often than pointing out concerns.

The same outlook toward ourselves is essential. We must recognize and believe in our strengths. A negative self-concept is damaging and limiting. Yes, we must realize we need to improve ourselves, believe others can help us become more like Jesus Christ, and commit ourselves to transforming action. But we must also know our skills, talents, gifts, and strengths so we will use them.

Without knowing our strengths, overcoming our challenges and compensating for weaknesses will be difficult, if not impossible. Knowing only our negatives often leads to believing lies about ourselves: No one wants me (belonging), I can't help anyone (purpose), and I can't do anything right (competence).

BUILDING
—ON—
THE ROCK

Before we go any further, turn back to your list of twenty statements. We'll work with them in this section.

▸ *First, so this exercise is truly beneficial, you may want to begin by praying that God will help you see the real you.*

▸ *Second, cross out statements that aren't currently true. Were you thinking too much about the past or the future?*

▸ *Third, to determine if your orientation is positive or negative, use one of the chart's columns to put plus signs behind true statements about your positive attributes and minus signs behind true statements about your weaknesses and sins. If your orientation was mainly negative, can you rewrite some of the statements more positively so you're more encouraged? For example, use adverbs and adjectives instead of nouns so conditions don't appear permanent. Maybe try rewriting statements right on the chart. Are there positive statements you can add that you didn't think of earlier? On the other hand, if your identity is too positive, try adding statements about some weaknesses to represent a more accurate description of yourself. Having almost all* negative or almost all positive statements is almost always a symptom of blind spots and/or pride.

▸ Fourth, decide if the category representation is complete and healthy. Did you narrowly define yourself, or are many categories represented? It's definitely okay to not have all eight categories included. You can use a chart column to match the statements with their categories (e.g., intellectual, emotional, social, character qualities, physical, career, material possessions, spiritual). Identities that don't fit a category can be designated by "other." For example, many missionary kids I've met in our international ministry might include "missionary kid" on their lists.

▸ Fifth, what do you think about the order of your statements? Is there a healthier order that better reflects how much weight each one holds? You can renumber them in the last column on the chart.

. . . .

REVISING
—THE—
DYNAMIC SEQUENCE

I've watched a lot of television coverage related to the events of September 11, 2001. I believe the interactive nature of this Model's components have probably played out often in the lives of those directly affected by the terrorism.

Security affects identity. Reflect on those who lost loved ones that day. The people who probably fared better are those with faith in God, a strong support system, and who knew they could independently make wise decisions. Their behavior (stemming from their security in God and identities of "I'm strong" and "I know God's loving care," for instance) caused others to know and describe them as strong individuals who relied on God in the midst of terrible circumstances.

Identity affects belonging and belonging affects identity, as I'll elaborate on in chapter 6. Parents who buried children met other grieving parents at support groups and formed strong emotional bonds. Men and women who lost their spouses on 9/11 have married each other. Children who lost parents like to spend time with other children experiencing the same loss because they understand each other's pain and fears. Such relationships can be healthy and healing. However, if people meet their belonging need only from those who share their 9/11/01 identity, then the identity of "sad parent," "grieving spouse," and "fearful child" might become so cemented that they remain sad, grieving, and fearful.

Identity and belonging influence purpose and competence. Many parents and spouses who lost loved ones that day discovered they had a new purpose for living. The same can be said for rescue workers and some government and airline employees. Nonprofit foundations have been formed that otherwise wouldn't have been. Committees meet to discuss and implement new security procedures. People who used to consider themselves ordinary citizens have taken up new causes and commitments.

And many of these individuals are finding skills and competencies they never knew they had. For example, I've heard several people say they didn't know they could give speeches. As we'll fully develop later in the book, authentic purpose leads to competence.

Destructive things can clarify our five core needs and show us if they're met in healthy ways. How do we respond during these times? Examining the strength of our first need, security, and the sources we rely on for it, is always a smart place to begin. Reestablishing security, or establishing it for the first time, can help us proceed all the way to competence. We'll know if all five are rooted in the Father, Son, and Holy Spirit, because we'll have authentic hope and wholeness. Authentic hope and wholeness in Christ feels quite different from hoping in ourselves or in other people and things here on earth.

I've learned (sometimes the hard way) that our five core

needs are also made abundantly obvious as a result of won-derfully energizing experiences. Just as with bad news, I try to examine my security immediately after getting excellent news. Otherwise, my tendency is to put my security only in myself (e.g., Look what I accomplished!) and/or those who impressed me (e.g., They'll keep making smart decisions!), rather than in God.

Is this a big deal? Yes it is, because my identity could easily become rooted in pride, and my behavior could become self-centered: "Notice me. Did you hear my news? Aren't I won-derful?" Because the components of the Model are linked, such unbiblical self-perception would then create a "domino downfall" of problems with my belonging, purpose, and com-petence. Can you see what the problems might be?

· ·

BUILDING
—ON—
THE ROCK

▸ *Based on what you read, think of two or more things you're grateful for understanding about identity.*
▸ *Which categories of your identity (e.g., intellectual, so-cial, etc.) do you perceive as strongest right now? Which area would you like to see significantly strengthened? Who can help you accomplish what's necessary for healthy changes to take root?*
▸ *Think of two or more questions you hope I answer in the next chapter about the change process.*
▸ *As I've written before, for hope and wholeness to be au-thentic, we need to anchor our thoughts and actions on God's Word. Therefore, you might want to spend some time reading and reflecting on the recommended Scrip-*

ture verses for chapter 4 that you'll find on the book's Web site: www.AuthenticHope.com.

. . . .

For as he thinketh in his heart, so is he.

–*Proverbs 23:7 KJV*

FIVE

THE CHANGE PROCESS

AS YOU'VE BEEN READING this book, have you thought of specific changes you'd like to make in your life? If I did not believe transformation was possible from negative to positive, unhealthy to healthy, weakness to strength, and sin to righteousness, I would not have written this book. This chapter is all about change as a practical life skill for strengthening identity.

Sometimes change can be crystallized quickly. Remember the example of Rachel at the beginning of chapter 4? This young girl chose to leave her interrupting behind. With some practical instruction and her parents' guidance, she changed in just a matter of days.

Other times, transformation requires that we establish new relationships so we're no longer influenced by people who behave like we used to. Also, people who have known us to be a certain way can have a hard time letting us change. Therefore, we need to connect with people who behave like we need to. (We'll explore this dimension of belonging early in the next chapter.)

Personal reform may be easier if we read different books, stop watching certain kinds of television and movies, listen to different CDs, and go to different stores. It all depends upon what we're trying to correct.

In order to experience change, we must have at least some control over the "thing" we want to change. This "thing" has to be changeable, unlike my height that I didn't like but couldn't alter. Also, we must truly desire something better for ourselves. You know what else I've discovered? *Wanting* to change is enough. When I wait until I need to, I'm so ensnared in the sin that it's more challenging. The desperation I feel is actually distracting and quitting is tempting. I'm learning to choose change before I have to.

Here's another absolute: prayer is essential. Seeking God continually makes a difference. We need to ask for His wisdom and His ways. Let's not stop there though. It's wise to involve prayer warriors, accountability partners, and selected family and friends. There's power in joining together (Esther 4:16; Matthew 18:20). We don't need to tell *all* our friends or prayer partners, but we will benefit from telling a few trustworthy people the specific sin we want to turn from.

Authentic transformation won't take root without Jesus mightily and lovingly transforming our identities from unsaved to saved, sinner to saint-who-sometimes-sins, and guilty to forgiven. Have you ever known this to be true in your life?

WHERE TO START

Through prayer and reading Scripture, we discover God's best for us. We are shown what it is and how to have it. As we rely on the empowering of the Holy Spirit working in us to do specific things, we can be successful in applying the powerful Word of God to our situations. I find Ephesians 4:22–24 to be a core passage for understanding the change process:

You were taught, with regard to your former way of life,
to put off your old self, which is being corrupted by its deceitful desires;
to be made new in the attitude of your minds;
and to put on the new self,
created to be like God in true righteousness and holiness.

Have you ever sought to put off your old self? Have you asked for prayer support to do it? That's a smart thing to do. But have you ever, much sooner than you expected, reverted back to your old self and given up? I have. It's discouraging. After one of these oh-too-frequent instances, I opened the Bible, hoping for some insight. That's when God showed me this Ephesians passage and parallel truth recorded in Colossians 3:9–10 and Romans 6. Applying the entire process has made the difference for me.

Permit an analogy before we get to the specifics. I live alone in what is for me the perfect little house on a quiet cul-de-sac in Fort Worth. When I get home after a long day or from a speaking trip, the first thing I want to do is change clothes. And I don't put comfortable clothes on over my business clothes. Also, I rarely change only part of my outfit, while leaving on the rest. I change completely. I take off my "old" clothes and put on something "new." (Before I do any of that, though, I take off my shoes—a high priority for me since I spend so much time on my feet!)

The change process works in a similar way. We are directed to put off our old selves. I think change is challenging because we don't change all the way around. Do you know people who put love on top of their anger, rather than removing the anger first? What happens when they are under stress? Their old self, the anger, most likely emerges. We must take the old self all the way off.

While already wearing a jacket, have you started to put on another one before realizing what you were doing? Many teens and adults who have heard me teach this change process have admitted they're wearing many layers—impatience, patience, impatience, patience, impatience, patience.

We can't just take off the old. Walking around with nothing on isn't comfortable either. However, we shouldn't just grab whatever's available without thinking. We need to pay attention. Have you ever left the house in your black slip, rather than in your black skirt? I know someone who has. Maybe you know someone who taught all day in one blue shoe and one brown shoe. I do. She admitted that if a student hadn't noticed, she probably wouldn't have.

We're wise to put on everything we need for the occasion for which we're getting dressed—nothing more and nothing less. What if we look in our closet and realize we don't have something we need? To change, we need access to something to change into, don't we? That's also the case when changing from our "former way of life" to our new way. The great news is that we know what we need to shop for because we're instructed in Ephesians 4:24 to put on "the new self, created to be like God." He is readily available to us!

From this Ephesians 4 passage (and supported by many other New Testament Scriptures), I believe we can lay out the transformation process in four stages:

Stage One	Recognize and put off an old, unrighteous identity and related behaviors, and choose and put on a new, righteous identity with corresponding behaviors.
Stage Two	Recognize lies; unbiblical motivators, values, desires, and attitudes; and strengths used badly.
Stage Three	Renew our minds to put off lies and put on truth.
Stage Four	Write out new belief statements that correspond to the reasons for our unrighteous behavior.

All this occurs with the empowerment of the Holy Spirit, the embrace of Father God's unconditional love, toward the goal of Christlike character.

. . . .

BUILDING
—ON—
THE ROCK

Before going further, you'll benefit from choosing one area in your life to transform. Try to choose something related either to how you interact with someone specific or a behavior pattern from your interactions with people in general. (For example, not responding with anger when your spouse is late, being more attentive when a child asks to show you something, or courageously answering *no* instead of *maybe* when you know your *maybe* actually means *no*.)

Choose only one issue for now. If you're aware of other negative identities or behaviors, you can apply this process to them later. I don't want you to get overwhelmed! Take some time to reflect and choose before continuing.

. . . .

STAGE ONE:
PUT OFF THE OLD, PUT ON THE NEW

Recognize and put off an old,
unrighteous identity and related behaviors,
AND choose and put on a new,
righteous identity with corresponding behaviors.

Change involves taking off the old and putting on the new. Trying to stop one behavior without thinking about what to replace it with doesn't work. That's why I've combined verses 22 and 24 of Ephesians 4 in this first stage of the change process. We'll be most successful when we decide, at the same time, what to put off (verse 22) and what to put on (verse 24).

By way of illustration, let's continue with the issue of interrupting, something with which I'm all too familiar. When I worked through this sin issue, my actual list of identities and observable behaviors looked like this:

Put Off Old Identity	Put On New Identity
"I'm an interrupter."	"I'm a listener who converses without interrupting."

Put Off Old Behavior	Put On New Behaviors
Interrupting	Wait until each person is finished talking. Prioritize the speaker by making eye contact. Concentrate more on what's being said. Make note of a key word to remember what I want to say.

I just listed one behavior I wanted God to help me remove. This is almost always best. For example, I could have included "not listening." That's clearly related to interrupting. But it involved what I was not doing. Instead, I stuck to one inappropriate action that I exhibited. (I think you'll see that related problems, like not listening, are usually dealt with as we continue the process. Then we'll realize which unrighteousness we need to attack next. For me, after going through all four stages with interrupting, it was impatience. I saw how linked they were and worked through it next.)[1]

Before we continue my example for stage 1, go ahead and list the old identity and corresponding behaviors you want to take off. (Because of the upcoming stages and how we'll analyze them, using pen and paper, rather than just thinking your thoughts, will be most profitable.) Then list some corresponding, righteous new behaviors.

You may find this task mentally or emotionally difficult. Take heart! Be patient with yourself. If the sin you want to eliminate is deeply entrenched, it's not always easy to know and live out the opposite conduct. I often wait in silence with my pen poised. I pray with the desire to be obedient to the leading of the Holy Spirit. He often shows me what I couldn't see on my own. It may be wise to involve an accountability partner or someone you know who will be thrilled you're working on this issue. Talking it out almost always leads to more conclusions.

Next, list the new identity you want to be known for. (This is often easier to do after you list the behaviors you want to adopt.)

STAGE TWO: IDENTIFY UNDERLYING REASONS

*Recognize lies; unbiblical motivators, values,
desires, and attitudes; and strengths used badly.*

I learned a long time ago that knowing what I should stop doing isn't enough to get me to stop. The list of new behaviors helps, but that isn't enough either. (For instance, many teenagers still choose to engage in sexual activity, even when they know how dangerous it can be and what righteous activities they could take part in instead.)

For the "putting off" and "putting on" to work the way God intended, we need to identify the core deceptions underlying our sinful behaviors. These can include lies that we believe and unbiblical motivators, values, desires, and attitudes. We must also identify any strengths we're using in unhealthy ways. Once we know the faulty foundations of our behaviors, we can revise, correct, and/or reject them.

Stage 1 involved recognizing unrighteous conduct and the righteous conduct that can replace it. The specific deceptions that are affecting us will become clear as we attempt to behave in new ways. When we find new behaviors awkward and anxiety producing, that may spark an internal confrontation with deeply rooted deceptions, such as a self-serving motivation, a prejudicial attitude, or a desire to receive recognition and glory that God deserves. (Ouch!)

Before we can totally put off our old self, we must accomplish stage 2 and recognize the foundational deceptions we believe. For example, to put off my interrupting, I had to face many questions. *Why don't I wait for others to finish their thoughts? Why don't I naturally prioritize the speaker? Why don't I listen better? What lies and unbiblical attitudes, desires, values, and/or motivators am I entangled by?*

Ultimately, our reasons and the lies they're rooted in must convert at the core in order for our behaviors to be continually transformed over time. This is true, no matter the unrighteous actions or deceit involved. Without recognizing the foundational deceptions and striving for transformation with the Spirit's empowerment, the changes won't last long term and the new desired behaviors won't become the norm.

Stage 2 in this change process involves listing the various reasons we behave as we do. Look at the old identity and behavior you wrote down as your own case study to examine. Now make a list of causes by asking yourself this question: Why do I do *this*?

Perhaps my actual, prayer-soaked list of reasons for interrupting will help you create your list. These statements rattled out of my brain and onto paper in exactly this order:

1. I quickly come up with ideas as I listen to others.
2. I believe ideas are important.
3. I believe my ideas are more important than theirs.
4. Talking gets me more attention than listening.
5. I want to encourage people by providing the solutions I come up with as I listen.
6. I believe others won't come up with my ideas.

You get the idea? Find your piece of paper and list lies you believe; ungodly attitudes, motivators, desires; and strengths that may also explain your behavior.

Were you humbled like I was? This isn't necessarily a fun process! I almost always have quick, gut reactions to what I see myself write down. Did you? Let me show you what I mean:

Reasons for Interrupting	Gut Reactions
1. I quickly come up with ideas as I listen to others.	Listen longer, Kathy.
2. I believe ideas are important.	Of course they are.
3. I believe my ideas are more important than theirs.	This is ugly! I need to believe other people can and will have valuable input.
4. Talking gets me more attention than listening.	Ouch! Why do I need attention? I should be giving attention, not trying to get it.
5. I want to encourage people by providing the solutions I come up with as I listen.	Even though people often thank me for my insights and input, I need to make sure I've heard everything relevant before I share.

Reasons for Interrupting	Gut Reactions
6. I believe others won't come up with my ideas.	This doesn't excuse my stepping on their words! And this is ugly— why do I assume my ideas are so valuable?

I've learned the hard way that quick reactions aren't deep enough in themselves to cause change. I've wanted to rely on them, but in doing so, I consistently keep behaving in damaging ways. We have to keep digging.

STAGE THREE: RENEW THE MIND

Renew our minds to put off deception and put on truth.

I hope this process makes sense and that my concrete example helps you think more deeply about your own issues. I've met many people who agree with me that change is challenging. Our results can still disappoint others and ourselves, even when we move between "I want to," "I need to," "I should," and "I must." But it doesn't all depend on us! It is crucial that we rely on the Holy Spirit during all four stages of this process. He will intervene to help us consider what's going on, illumine the issues so we can learn, and empower us to behave righteously. Hang in there!

Discarding outward behavior (stage 1) and discovering the underlying causes of our unbiblical behaviors (stage 2) are huge steps toward healing. But we still need stage 3, to renew our minds. We find this principle in the middle verse of the passage we've been using: "to be made new in the attitude of your minds" (Ephesians 4:23).

We must renew our minds so we can rightly use our strengths, put off the deception, and replace it with truth. This renewing is not done with Oprah, Dr. Phil, the horoscope, or escaping at the movies. As I understand it, renewing of the mind cannot done primarily with this book, even though the instruction is, I hope, helpful. Renewing the mind comes about by getting to know God's love, His mind, and His best for His children. Renewal is all about spiritual vitality, which we'll get from God through His presence and His Word.

Our passage gives us an "answer key" of sorts in verse 24: "The new self is to be like God." Knowing God doesn't just provide us with security. It also strengthens our true identity, because it allows us to discern what's wrong and what's right about ourselves. Comparing myself to my loving Father is always humbling and instructive. My knowledge of God and His ways is how I knew which of my motives for interrupting were sinful and which were not.

The intent of stage 3 is to renew our minds so we can fully reject the lies and claim new beliefs in stage 4. (Thankfully, Scripture shows us how to exchange something that's wrong for something that's right!) To renew, or transform, the mind, we'll engage in three activities that may take a bit of time and study. They'll result in a huge payoff though!

- First, we'll *process the reasons,* with a goal of discovering relevant topics to study in Scripture. We do this by determining deeper connections between our past behaviors and our underlying reasons. For example, we'll go beyond the fact that some reasons are sinful and we'll ask God to reveal which particular sins are involved. While doing this, we'll make some initial decisions that begin the renewal process.
- Second, we'll *dig into God's Word* with the discovered topics in mind. For example, if we've engaged in interrupting, we may realize we need to study patience, gentleness, wisdom, and guarding the tongue as resolutions to our reasons. The three categories of Scripture I'll recommend should help you intentionally uncover specific passages of relevant, life-changing truth.
- Third, we'll pursue *praying and repenting.* Processing the deception and reading Scripture that addresses our sin will give us plenty to talk about with God! Praying for His insights and wanting to respond obediently to them is mature; so is wanting to change. Frankly, sometimes sin is easy for me and behaving like Christ is hard. But repentance is right. Obedient choices allow us to benefit from God's best for us. Without repentance

and obedience, there's a barrier between God and us, and our fate will be spiritual listlessness rather than spiritual vitality.

You may choose to involve others in stage 3. I know of families who worked on issues together and ended up with a month's worth of family devotions. I also know husbands and wives who worked independently for a while and then came together to compare conclusions. Afterward, they continued studying together for a rich experience. Don't hesitate to do what you can, both individually and relationally, to make this process work for you.

Processing Reasons

After the statements are out on paper, I almost always reorganize them into categories to facilitate analysis. Sometimes they rattle out of my brain already in categories, but they didn't this time. In my list, lies 3 and 6 and motivator number 4 were due to sin. Statements 1 and 2 were due to the type of mind I have and my spiritual gift of teaching, and number 5 was related to my heart and spiritual gift of exhortation. So here's the list again, this time organized to facilitate further analysis:

Source	Kathy's Reasons in That Category
Because of My Sin	3. I believe my ideas are more important than theirs. 4. Talking gets me more attention than listening. 6. I believe others won't come up with my ideas.
Because of My Mind/Spiritual Gift of Teaching	1. I quickly come up with ideas as I listen to others. 2. I believe ideas are important.
Because of My Heart/Spiritual Gift of Exhortation	5. I want to encourage people by providing the solutions I come up with as I listen.

First, I determined that reasons number 3 (I believe my ideas are more important than theirs) and number 6 (I believe others won't come up with my ideas) were related, so I examined them together. I discerned that their root was pride. I dug further to see that it was specifically an issue of intellectual pride. I realized that my renewed beliefs would need to be oriented toward humility, specific to intellectual insights. Therefore, my initial thoughts based on past experiences, and knowledge of God and Scripture, included:

- I have a lot to learn, and many people can teach me.
- I am as important as others (not more or less important) and the same thing is true of my ideas.
- All God's children are capable of good ideas as we depend on Him and His wisdom. Those who aren't His followers can have good ideas that resonate with God's wisdom.

Second, I examined reason number 4 (Talking gets me more attention than listening). Unlike the above two statements, this statement is true. Talking gets all of us more attention than listening. But that's bad motivation! The root is similar; it's pride, with a self-centered twist. Talking more than listening is based on what I think I deserve—to be heard, acknowledged, appreciated, etc. The previous reasons were based on what I thought others deserved—namely, my brilliant ideas! (We'll only see such fine discriminations when we slow down and choose to examine ourselves. Prayer and godly counsel help.) These were my initial thoughts on this reason:

- God pays attention to me and is aware of my every thought and feeling. This needs to be enough for me.
- God did not create anyone else so they had to meet my need for feeling valuable. This is a legitimate need, but I need to meet it in healthy ways, primarily through Jesus Christ.
- I need balance in my communication. It's not wrong to talk, and it's not right only to listen. Both talking and listening are good. God does both, and so should we, but in right measure. This requires wisdom to know which goes when. I need to check my motives. Am I talking to gain attention for myself, or am I seek-

ing to build people up by sharing something that meets their legitimate needs? Am I willing to strengthen my ideas through other people's input? Asking these questions on a regular basis keeps me oriented toward humility.

Third, I spent time reflecting and praying about the three causes for my interrupting that aren't rooted in sin: I quickly come up with ideas as I listen to others, I believe ideas are important, and I want to encourage people by providing the solutions I come up with as I listen.

There's nothing wrong with being able to think of ideas quickly, to think ideas are important, or to want to encourage people with ideas. However, these inherent, God-given strengths become weaknesses when used excessively. (This is the case with virtually every strength. Too much of a good thing isn't a good thing.) For example, encouraging people happens to be among my spiritual gifts, but that doesn't mean I should interrupt in order to exhort. Strengths can lead to sin when we aren't attentive to that possibility. Therefore, I committed to pray regularly that God would prevent me from using my strengths badly.

Are you willing to give this process a try with your reasons in mind? Look at your reasons for the behavior you are focusing on, paying close attention to the sin issues involved. Look to see if any are related so you can analyze them together. Can you then identify the opposite belief(s)? (For example, in my case, pride was a significant root, and the opposite, Christlike quality is humility.) If you already know some truths from Scripture relevant to the sin root and opposite righteous quality, list those. If you don't discern anything, that's okay. Move on to the beliefs rooted in your strengths.

Is your pattern similar to mine? Do you have other categories? Allow me to suggest that if your list doesn't include sin, you may want to reexamine the reasons behind your behavior. (Do you remember anything about blind spots from the previous chapter? Our familiarity and warped sense of comfort with unrighteous practices can make it almost impossible to recognize some of the reasons behind them.) If you think you may have blind spots, could you call a trusted friend or relative to help you more fully process this?

Evidence of blind spots shows up in Stage 1. For example, if you study the list of new behaviors I said I needed to put on, you'll see that they're radically different from the actual changes I needed to make.

Digging into God's Word

After analyzing my reasons for interrupting, I turned to God's Word for the real renewal process. For example, based on my processing, I knew to look for verses about humility, listening, God's wisdom, teachability, and prioritizing other people.

There may be times when there isn't much revealed during the initial analysis. It depends upon how familiar we are with the Word and how many experiences we've had with the sin issues. And our choice to be vulnerable is a huge variable. Are we truly willing to identify our sin? Even when we begin our Scripture study with less information than I have here, God will influence time spent in His Word. During our study and accompanying prayer times, God's Spirit enables us to put off lies and unbiblical attitudes, desires, values, and motivators and put on truth.

I consistently find three key Scripture sources especially valuable when pursuing renewal of the mind for any specific issue: (1) God's behavior, character, and instruction; (2) wisdom from Proverbs, Psalms, and the New Testament; and (3) the "one-another" passages of the New Testament. Let me share how I used each of these to work through my issue of interrupting.

(1) The Triune God's Behavior, Character, and Instruction

We can usually find something in the person and work of Jesus Christ that is very relevant to our issues, whatever they may be. This includes the words of Christ, descriptions of His character by the Scripture's writers, and indications of how Christ relates with us today. We find righteousness that we can emulate. Something about God and the Holy Spirit will often relate directly to our struggle, as well.

I could not find a verse that commands, "Thou shalt not interrupt!" And yet, it's clear that interrupting is not God honoring in most situations. I frequently found that Christ exhibited the positive counter-behavior. He listened carefully, then responded with comments or questions that showed He was both listening and interested in people's opinions. (For an example, see His interaction with the woman at the well in John 4.) Also, His actions were never self-serving, even when they drew attention, like when He confronted the money changers in the temple.

As I considered my interrupting, I was especially encouraged by these verses: Genesis 1:27; Micah 6:8; Matthew 23:12; Philippians 2:5, 8; and Colossians 2:3.

(2) Proverbs, Psalms, and New Testament Truth

I frequently search Proverbs, a book of wisdom. I'm never disappointed because the instruction is practical, positive, and timely. Although I highly recommend going right to the Bible to find relevant truth, some authors have categorized the Proverbs in helpful ways. You may want to consider investing in a book like this.[2]

Studies in the Psalms also enrich the renewing of the mind. They were often used to worship God in the temple and synagogues before the coming of Christ and are still used today to glorify God. Praising God today with Psalms reveals vital truths and is humbling. God regularly uses my attempts to praise Him, both privately and corporately in church, to show me sin I wasn't aware of.

Paul, James, Peter, and other writers of the New Testament recorded God's wisdom too. Going right to Scripture is extremely beneficial, but at times, books with Scripture categorized for us can be helpful. John Kruis has done this for eighty-one topics, using passages from the Old Testament (including Proverbs) and New Testament.[3] Also, the "Biblical Counseling Keys" from June Hunt's ministry, *Hope for the Heart,* never disappoint me.[4] They're dynamite!

Here are the verses that helped me. If you take the time to look some of them up and read them, you'll see their relevance to the beliefs I once held. Psalm 111:10; Proverbs 3:34; 9:9; 11:2; 12:15; 15:33; 16:18; 18:13; 28:26; Romans 8:8; Philippians 2:3; James 1:5, 19; and 4:10.

(3) The "One Anothers" of the New Testament

For me, the "one-another" statements found in the New Testament serve as the third consistent source of both motivation and instruction. For instance, we are told to "accept one another," "honor one another," and "teach one another." It's rare when these statements aren't relevant to whatever renewal-of-the-mind issue I'm struggling with. Although these "one-another" instructions were meant to direct believers' actions and attitudes with other believers, we can apply them to all interactions. Since they're based on how Christ related with people, intentionally choosing to live them out helps us become more like Him and demonstrate His character to all people.

The "one-another" instructions also serve as a humbling evaluation tool. They help me answer these questions: "Is my mind being renewed? Am I behaving more frequently and more completely like Jesus Christ would have in this situation?"

Here are the specific "one anothers" I applied to my concern about interrupting:[5] Romans 12:10; 14:12–13; Galatians 5:26; Ephesians 4:2; 1 Thessalonians 4:18.

What do you think about this purposeful way of searching and studying the Bible? Are you encouraged or discouraged? Looking forward to trying it, or overwhelmed and unsure? Will you involve others, or does quiet time alone with God seem best for you? If you've thought of a fourth renewal source, go for it!

No matter how it seems now, this does not need to be a time-consuming process. And we don't need to do it all in one sitting. I often take many opportunities within a week to ponder, pray, and search because I find short amounts of time are usually more profitable than one extended session. Your knowledge of Scripture will certainly influence how easy it will be for you. It's actually fun—I enjoy searching Scripture with a purpose in mind! And with each verse I find, my hope deepens for achieving the goal God sets out before all of us, to become increasingly more like Jesus Christ (Romans 8:29).

Pursuing Prayer and Repentance

Prayer and repentance tend to be ongoing, continual elements of the change process. Praying for wisdom from God and for a humble heart of obedience throughout this process is vital for me. It's only in His love and strength that repentance is possible. Therefore, prayer is essential for us to turn things around. I try to pause and pray often as God reveals truth (I see sin for what it is) and I sense conviction from the Holy Spirit. I also prioritize prayer and repentance here in stage 3.

To repent, I confess the sin to God, rather than trying to excuse it away. I turn to God (not *toward* God, but hopefully all the way *to* God), seeking His change in my life from evil to good, sin to righteousness, and foolishness to wisdom. For example, from the sin of intellectual pride to teachability, from notice-me pride to humility, and from self-centeredness to putting others first. I want to change from an interrupter to a listener. Therefore, repenting from these sins is essential. It's only then that new beliefs and behaviors can become the norm.

My prayers tend to focus more on the future than the past: on who I am becoming more than who I've been. I ask for forgiveness and refreshment. I pledge more consistent and stronger obedience to the Spirit's leading as I ask God for more of His wisdom and His Spirit's strength to do what's right and to be who God wants me to be.

What about feeling sorry for my sins? Are you surprised I didn't include it as a part of repentance? It's not always there. Paul wrote that "godly sorrow brings repentance that leads to salvation and leaves no regret" (2 Corinthians 7:10). Godly sorrow can motivate us to repent. But with or without these feelings, when I know from my understanding of Scripture that I've sinned, repentance is the obedient response. Quite frankly, if I always waited to feel badly about my behavior, I'd repent much less frequently. Comparing my life to God's Word is the standard, not whether I feel badly about falling short.

So being in the Word and knowing the difference between obedience and disobedience is crucial. Otherwise, it will be almost impossible to know if we've grieved His Spirit (Ephesians 4:30). When my prayers of repentance are sincere, He cleanses my troubled mind and revives my heart (Psalm 34:18; Isaiah 57:15). Praise Him! Sometimes I experience instant relief, and at other times, it's more of a process. Perhaps I have more steps to take to get entirely out of the valley. I sometimes repeat, "Keep walking, don't sit down, keep walking, don't sit down."6

Sometimes I want to resist change and just stop after finishing the first two stages. Not only does stage 3 take time; the conviction I experience from it isn't fun. However, eventually, I'm grateful for it.

It won't help us much to stop after recognizing how we've been deceived. We must keep going. In the end, the process is definitely more encouraging than discouraging. It's worth the time. Hang in there with me, and I think you'll agree.

STAGE FOUR: WRITE OUT NEW BELIEFS

*Write out new belief statements that correspond
to the reasons for our unrighteous behavior.*

I conclude the change process by revisiting the list of reasons I was doing what I was doing, trying to keep all my progress in mind. I spent some time rewriting the reasons. In this stage, I include as much of a "redemptive edge" to the reasons for my behavior as possible. If they were sin-based, I focus on what the righteous behavior would be. If they were strength-based, I focus on how to use them in an appropriate, balanced way.

I write out these new ideas, rather than just think them, because writing requires a deeper level of processing. And seeing them in print makes them more real for me. I also read them out loud to myself periodically, usually for several weeks, for the same reason. Most importantly, I keep in communication with God throughout this process. Prayer matters!

I may also revisit my behavior list from stage 1 to add new righteous behaviors to it that God revealed during the renewal process. This is helpful when my convictions are slow in coming and what I've listed at the beginning of the change process isn't enough to revolutionize my actions.

To continue with my example, here's my new belief list. As with everything else I've shown you, this is exactly how I wrote my new statements:

1. Ideas are important, and I'm grateful to God for my mind that quickly processes information. For this to be a strength, I must let people complete their thoughts. I'm more likely to do this when I believe I have something to gain from their insights. I do! I'll like having a broader pool of ideas. Since I'm "people smart," other people's ideas stimulate my thoughts. And they're more likely to listen to me willingly when I've listened to them. My listening and teachability strengthens my position as "teacher," one of my passions.

2. Other people are capable of coming up with important ideas. If they're the same as mine, we will benefit from that affirmation. If they're different, I need to not quickly assume they're inferior to mine or irrelevant to the issue we're discussing. When I don't immediately see the strength of someone's idea, if it appears safe to do so, I will ask them to keep talking about it. Usually, with more information, I'll get the connections and see strengths I missed initially.

3. When I share unique ideas others haven't thought of, I need to do it in such a way that I don't make anyone feel less intelligent or less creative just because they didn't think of what I did. It has very little to do with intelligence or creativity and a lot to do with how much experience we've had with the topic, how relevant it is to us, how fascinated we are by it, and how much time we've spent daydreaming about it.

4. I'm grateful for the spiritual gifts of exhortation and teaching. I'm grateful God has allowed me to serve Him and others through these gifts. I must remember that listening and learning also encourage people. I'm grateful for the abilities to listen and learn.

5. I need to meet my need for feeling valuable and significant by reflecting on God's sacrifice of His Son on my behalf and not

by talking more than listening. When I sense I'm seeking people's attention in unhealthy ways, I need to apologize to them and turn to God.

6. In all of this, as with everything else, I must be motivated by my desire to please and glorify God—not so people are impressed with me or like me more.

. . . .

BUILDING
—ON—
THE ROCK

Renewal of the mind works, but don't just take my word for it. I sincerely hope and pray what I've written both motivates and equips you to apply the process to your own situations. In fact, I'd recommend you take some time right now to renew your mind through the active, personal, and instructive Word of God. Rely on the Holy Spirit to lead and empower you.

If that seems overwhelming to you now, that's understandable. It's a humbling experience—and yet so very rich! Perhaps after a break, you'll be up to the challenge. If you choose not to do so now, when will you begin the process? Maybe you can commit a specific time to do so and share that decision with someone you trust. May the triune God bless you as you pursue renewal of your mind in Him!

. . . .

*Since, then, we do not have
the excuse of ignorance, everything–
and I do mean everything–connected
with that old way of life has to go.
It's rotten through and through.
Get rid of it!*

And then take on an
entirely new way of life–
a God-fashioned life,
a life renewed from the inside
and working itself into your conduct
as God accurately reproduces
his character in you.

–*Ephesians 4:22-24 THE MESSAGE*

SIX

BELONGING
Who Wants Me?

I'VE GAINED WEIGHT over the past several years. I used to be in great shape. Throughout high school and college, I enjoyed intramural sports. And before my two knee surgeries in the early '80s, I played racquetball often. Perhaps you can relate to a lifestyle and metabolism change that results in dreaded weight gain.

I've only recently felt truly ready and able to lose the pounds I need to. What made the difference? Belonging.

My mom brings up my weight almost every time we communicate —on the phone, via e-mails, when we're together. I'm grateful that she's not mean about it. I know she's motivated by love and the fact that my dad passed away from a heart attack, in which diabetes and weight were contributing factors. Her concern intensified when she was diagnosed with cancer. Out of my love and respect for her, I've wanted to lose weight. But for some reason, my mom's concern wasn't enough.

A TEAM EFFORT

As it turns out, God used eight other people in six different ways to help me lose weight: role modeling, joining me, accountability, encouraging, instructing, and praying. This expanded sense of belonging has made all the difference.

Role Modeling

Our office manager, Joyce, got serious about losing weight. She and her doctors hoped it would result in less pain in her back and legs and lower blood pressure. I've admired her self-discipline and perseverance and noticed how much healthier she looks.

Using a different system, Linda, our administrative assistant, also lost weight. She's smiling more these days and clearly feels better about herself.

I first learned about Lamar's weight loss in an e-mail. I saw him a few months later and was instantly impressed. I hardly recognized him. He looked fabulous, appeared even more confident, and obviously had energy to spare. I was inspired by him since he is also a speaker and teacher—and if he could do it in his circumstances, I realized that I could do it in mine. This dimension of his role modeling was important.

Joining Me

God used Jalisa to give me a book. I thought, *not another book about losing weight!* Other friends I love and respect had done that, but most of these books went unread. This time was different, because Jalisa was using the author's recommendations herself. We could do the program together.

Accountability

Then Aisha entered the picture. Because she is one of my accountability partners, I e-mailed her that I had gotten serious—again— about losing weight. Her e-mail response included a request for more information about the book Jalisa and I had so she could get it and join us on our journey. Her commitment to me is strong, so her choice didn't surprise me, and I was grateful for her support.

I knew it would help to be honest with Aisha because I'd see her two months later. This type of accountability works better for me than just relying on phone calls and e-mails. It would have been less risky to keep quiet about it. She would have been pleasantly surprised by any weight loss and, if I hadn't lost weight, she wouldn't have known to be disappointed. But I knew telling her would increase my chance for success.

Encouraging

I still remember a positive encounter with Tara. I'd just returned from a speaking trip, so we hadn't seen each other for about ten days. After we greeted, she smiled broadly: "Kathy, it's obvious you've lost weight!" Her encouragement helped me stay the course.

Instructing

Because of comments Eva made, I knew she wanted to lose weight. When I saw her six months later, her weight loss was obvious. Because we had been vulnerable during earlier conversations, I knew I could ask her how she did it. Through her, I found a method that has worked.

Praying

I mentioned my increasing desire to lose weight as an example during a convention presentation. I asked people to pray for me. One woman said that she could relate to my struggle. She continued, "I'm going to pray specifically that your taste in food will change, and that the food you crave you will no longer crave." I was speechless. I don't even know her name, and yet she loved me in a very personal and practical way.

God brings this woman to mind at the most frustrating times—like when I'm tempted with Pepperidge Farm Mint Milano cookies! If I walk down the grocery store cookie aisle, I often glance in the direction of the Milanos, check out the price, and think about getting a bag or two. Then her prayer pops into my head. I think that if she cares enough to pray that prayer, it would be immature and irresponsible for me to buy these cookies. It would demonstrate a lack of faith in God! I pass them by (usually) because I know someone prays specifically about this element of weight loss. Her prayers strengthen my belonging. And when I do choose to purchase these favorite cookies (I'm such a sucker for mint!), the bag lasts longer than it used to.

At this writing, I've lost twenty-eight pounds. I want—no, I need—to lose more. I'm very encouraged, though, because losing the first pounds has never been easy. When I've tried before and not lost weight, I've quickly given up. This time, my desire was intensified by my mom's legitimate concerns. How could I be concerned about her health but appear to be unconcerned about mine? It bordered on hypocrisy.

My identity is no longer, "I want to lose weight," "I need to lose weight," or even, "I should lose weight." It has changed to, "I am losing weight." This shift was possible because my behaviors changed. These behavior changes and small, but significant, identity changes resulted from the different ways my belonging need was met. Rather than believing, "I'll never be able to lose weight," I knew "I can lose weight."

The cycle continues. Now, my new identity of "I am losing weight" continues to positively influence my beliefs and behaviors. When in restaurants, I ask servers to not bring me any bread. This is huge for me! During my elementary and junior high years, my dad worked at Red Star Yeast in Milwaukee. Once a week, he brought home a fresh-baked loaf of bread. Therefore, fresh, hot bread has always been a stumbling block for me. Exhibiting self-control in this area is an accomplishment. I am grateful to God!

The identity shift about weight was sparked by my belonging. Other than the mystery prayer warrior, I've known these friends for years and my mom for my whole life. But these relationships took on new power as we connected around this one issue. That's how belonging and camaraderie work.

BUILDING
—ON—
THE ROCK

What about you? Is there something you're trying to improve about yourself and this illustration helped you realize you may be trying to do it alone or without as many people as might be best? If so, what is it? I advise you to write down some of the answers to these questions and make this idea of change more concrete and less hypothetical.

▸ *List names of some current or potential helpers.*
▸ *When will you contact them to help you?*
▸ *What would be wise prayer requests?*

JOB'S TOXIC FRIENDS

I wish all connections were positive. I've had a few personal and professional relationships that started very well, but ended up toxic. Friends who know the history of these situations have asked if I've regretted getting involved with these people. The answer has always been no. I'm grateful for the good times and what I've learned through the experiences, but I'm also grateful they're behind me.

We can learn from both positive and negative examples. In the book of Job, we have both. If you're not familiar with Job, his story is recorded in a book that bears his name. It's found just before the book of Psalms, near the middle of the Bible. Many believe it's a book about suffering, but it's really more a book about faith. Therefore, if security in God is an issue for you, I recommend reading Job to find examples of his trust in a trustworthy God.

We learn something about Job's identity from Job 1:1: "Job . . . was blameless and upright; he feared God and shunned evil." Yet God allowed great suffering to come upon his life. He lost his wealth, ten children died in one gust of wind, his wife mocked him, and he became very ill.

We learn something of Job's security when we read Job 1:21. After these catastrophes, he said, "May the name of the LORD be praised." That gets a "Wow!" response from me. Even though Job's life changed drastically, he didn't blame God, so his identity in Him remained solid.

In the midst of his trauma, four of Job's friends showed up. Did they help him? Not really. They did do something right after hearing of Job's plight—they went to sit with him in silence and grieve his losses. But after a time of silence, three of the four began sharing their skewed analysis of his situation. Where my friends encouraged me, Job's friends discouraged him. Where a woman prayed to God on my behalf, his friends talked about God in ways that weren't positive. Where my friends modeled success in my same weight situation, his were unwilling to identify with his circumstances. Jalisa and Aisha walked with me; Job's friends stood against him.

What a sad reality. Job's friends began with good motives but ended up dragging him down. Where my healthy belonging resulted in hope, his unhealthy belonging caused some despair.

For many reasons, I'm humbled by Job's example. Here's just one way: Although he was treated badly by these four supposed friends, it's not recorded in the book that he was anything but the best of friends to them. Near the end of the book, God Himself tells Job that his friends were wrong and would be judged and destroyed unless Job interceded on their behalf. Job willingly prays so they are spared. That's worth another "Wow!" I want to be a person who prays when confronted with difficult people.

WHEN WE'RE TOXIC

But what about when we are the friends who are unhealthy or unpleasant? This slice of Job's life reminds me of a challenging time in my own past with my friend Emily. (Do you remember her from chapter 1?)

I praise God Emily valued our friendship enough to communicate a concern she had about me. She sent me a letter. (I'm an advocate of using the written word. It's more believable and it forces the writer to think things through, provide evidence for anything negative, and suggest specific changes and solutions. Also, written input allows the reader to respond privately and then think deeply before writing back, calling, or talking face-to-face. I don't recommend it as a substitute for discussions, but it's often a safe and smart way to begin when tough issues are involved.) Emily eloquently and carefully explained that our friendship was at risk because she often felt like a project I was trying to finish or a problem I wanted to fix. Rather than analyzing her, she asked me to love her.

I wasn't aware how I was coming across, but I saw it as soon as she called me on it. I can easily analyze people and help them solve their problems, but as I've written, anything well done, overdone, is badly done. Our friendship began with Emily wanting and needing my insights, but she had gained a healthy perspective and was learning to think on her own. She was no longer the same person. Now she needed me to listen, not analyze. I, therefore, needed to change and learn how to demonstrate my love and care in different ways.

I independently worked through some issues, apologized to her, repented (changed directions), and chose to work on new behaviors. Also, Emily provided me with additional insights, and we worked through some aspects of our relationship together. Our friendship became stronger than ever. For instance, now, before I call Emily, I often ask God to help me listen well and speak less. When I believe I have an insight, I sometimes ask if she wants me to share or if she wants more time to problem solve on her own. I do the same with a few other people too. This helps make me a more trustworthy friend, improves our security, helps reinforce positive identity, and strengthens belonging.

TOXIC FAMILY SITUATIONS

I do pray that adults consider the short-term and long-term ramifications of their decisions and actions, which can easily affect all five needs of their peers and protégés. Which brings up the story of Emily again.

Do you remember from chapter 1 that Emily was sexually abused by her father and her mother was emotionally distant? Emily's resulting performance mind-set and eating disorder played havoc with her life for years—and they still raise their ugly heads every now and then. In addition, the abuse also affected Emily's relationship with her husband, Art.

Because of the way Emily was raised, she and Art weren't sure it was wise to have children. After prayer and counsel, they did, and they don't regret it. Emily's perfectionistic tendencies and her mom's emotional abandonment are sometimes on her mind as she interacts with her two precious daughters. (Their third is already in heaven with Jesus.) I wish she didn't have such concerns. If her five core needs had been met in healthy ways when she was a child, I think it would have spared her much suffering.

Have you discovered, though, how much you can learn from negative examples? Emily did by reflecting on her own past and working through issues of forgiveness and transformation. As a result, Emily is very connected emotionally with Rosalie and Sherika. She's also very aware of who their friends are, and she has established open lines of communication. Also Emily obediently sacrifices for them. For example, I was proud of her when she enrolled in swim classes with Rosalie and Sherika. The "old" Emily struggled with her body image, so she would never go swimming, since that meant being seen in a bathing suit. Likewise, she never wanted her picture taken. Yet because of the girls, now Emily allows photos to be taken of herself and even shares them with friends. She admits that it's not easy. I'm proud of her because she's doing what's right, not what's easy. Emily and Art credit God for healing and helping them. They're motivated to love their daughters well and rely on God's wisdom and the Holy Spirit's leading and empowerment to do so.

LIFE SKILL: FRIENDSHIP

Belonging has numerous dimensions, doesn't it? There are the people—family, friends, coworkers, acquaintances—and the reality that these relationships can be healthy and constructive or toxic and destructive. I could have chosen any number of issues as the belonging life skill. I decided to focus on friendship because understanding its complexity may lead to more fulfilling relationships and healthier belonging.

To Be, or Not to Be?

After speaking about this Model to children and teens, audience members frequently ask questions about belonging.[1] This is one of the most common: "Dr. Kathy, my mom and dad told me not to be friends with this kid. But I did anyway. Now I know they were right, but I don't know how to get rid of this guy. What should I do?"

Here's another common scenario. I thank students who look out for peers who seem lonely. I thank them if they reach out to the kid on the playground who seems alone, the one who's always chosen last, or the one who eats by himself or herself. I also thank teachers who notice children who struggle to belong and do something about it. Because I share these comments, students sometimes ask me this type of question: "Dr. Kathy, I always eat lunch with the same three or four girls. Well, there's this new girl I think is nice, and I asked her to eat with us. But my friends don't want to add anybody to the group. So, like, I don't know what to do. Can I make them accept her? Should I stop eating with them and eat with the new girl? But then my old friends will be upset, and they might stop being my friends. What do you think I should do?"

Friendships aren't always smooth sailing, are they? I think too many of us treat friendship issues lightly and flippantly. Do we have the courage to look squarely at our attitudes and behaviors (influenced by our identity) and change where necessary? Then do we come alongside friends to help them change as I described in chapter 5?

Here, as the belonging life skill, I'll offer a list of friendship categories and suggest practical questions to help us identify our own needs, as well as needs others have. As with the change process in chapter 5, if we think through these issues with ourselves in mind first, we'll gain credibility and expertise to help others.

Getting the Big Picture

Before we launch into more details, let me first sketch a big picture of friendship. It relies on two cycles. One involves the process of beginning a casual relationship, and from there moving into a close friendship, and then to (possibly) a committed friendship.[2] We relate differently with each cluster of friends:

Casual friends: People we occasionally see. We might want to know them better.

Close friends: People we regularly see. We might want to know them better, or, because of conflict or other issues, we might want to shift these relationships back to the casual level from time to time.

Committed friends: People we count on for help and great joy. We may sometimes struggle with them, but the dedication remains. (Emily and I were in this category. We still are!)

Another friendship cycle involves various stages within that process: self-evaluation, conversation skills, choosing friends wisely, maintaining relationships and resolving conflicts, and ending relationships when appropriate. Dynamic friendships balance both cycles so there is natural progression in the level of trust and involvement and movement within each stage so a friendship stays fresh. To make the sections below more meaningful, you might want to reflect on friendship struggles you've had before.

Self-Evaluation
- Is there anything about me that might cause others to avoid choosing me as a friend? Sin issues? Irritating habits? Lack of interest or knowledge resulting in boring conversations? Something else?
- If it is something that can be changed, how can I do so?
- If something can't be changed, how can I change my own attitude so it's less of an issue?
- Can I emphasize strengths without being prideful? Or do my strengths somehow get in the way?
- Should I ask others if they think there's something about me that's causing problems? If so, who am I secure enough to trust?

Conversation Skills

- What questions might people ask me to start conversations? How can I answer them?
- What questions can I ask others to start conversations? What follow-up questions could I have ready? How would I answer the same questions if they asked me?
- What can I talk about that others might find interesting?
- Other than talking, what else could I do to connect with people? (For instance, stand up to greet them, shake hands, make eye contact, etc.)
- Should I ask for help so I can interact better?

Choosing Friends Wisely

- What types of people do I most want to be friends with?
- Who would be a good influence on me? Who would I enjoy getting to know?
- What qualities should I look for?
- How will I know which people have those qualities?
- How can I be sure to give people a fair chance instead of quickly rejecting them?
- How can I appropriately respond to my feelings of loneliness?
- Are there clubs or organizations I can join so I'll meet people I might want to connect with?
- Should I ask for help on choosing friends more wisely?

Maintaining Relationships and Resolving Conflicts

- What can I do if a relationship becomes boring?
- When friends and I have problems, how can I know if it's my fault and I need to change?
- How do I know when to ask for forgiveness because of something I've done? How should I ask? What should I do if people say they won't or can't forgive me?
- Should I tell others when I think our friendship problems are their fault? If so, how?
- When I've been hurt, should I tell people? How do I forgive them? How do I know if I can trust them again?
- Is compromising so there's less conflict ever appropriate? If so, when? When is it not?
- Should I ask for help in maintaining relationships and resolving conflict?

Ending Relationships When Appropriate

- How do I decide a relationship is no longer healthy?
- If I determine it needs to end, how do I appropriately end it? Do I need to tell people we can't be friends or can I just stop talking with and doing things with them?
- If I know a friendship is unhealthy but I don't want it to end, what does that say about me? What need do I need to meet in other ways?
- How should I respond if this friend doesn't want to end the friendship or won't stop contacting me?
- Should I ask for help in ending relationships?

IDENTITY AND PURPOSE MATTER!

From what you understand about the interlocking sequence of components in the Model, can you predict how a faulty identity influences belonging? You might want to think your prediction through before reading on.

I'll share some of my thoughts about how counterfeit identities can influence belonging. A narrow (or incomplete) identity almost always limits growth because it restricts whom we choose to connect with. For example, children who define themselves entirely by their physical abilities and interests, may only want to participate in and talk about sports. (Many narrow identities are possible.)

People with inaccurate identities believe they're one thing when they're actually another. Often this identity is falsely positive. For instance, they think they're leaders, but others think of them as being bossy. Maybe they believe they are knowledgeable, but they come across as arrogant. Such people may struggle to fit in. Not belonging well with those they believe they have something in common with can be especially devastating. And since they perceive some of their weaknesses as strengths (e.g., leadership or knowledge), they won't seek people who can help them improve, and they'll probably resent anyone who tries.

Do you enjoy interacting with negative people? Probably not, which is why it's easy to see that those with negative identities will almost always struggle to have healthy belonging. They may be drawn to other negative people, which makes it harder for them to grow and mature. Positive people may steer clear of them, which leaves them feeling rejected. This almost always reinforces their negative thought patterns.

Moving on to purpose, how do you believe an unhealthy purpose influences belonging? For example, if our purpose is to be the best, we'll only want to be friends with a person if we think we are better than they are. And big egos and attempts at one-upmanship make healthy relationships difficult.

FINDING OUR BELONGING IN GOD

I'm glad you're still reading—looking at so many potential negatives can be draining! Now we'll see the best part! It's wrong to depend on others to meet a need that God is designed to meet. Great people skills and quality friendships aren't enough. God meets our belonging need. As our Creator, He has a claim on every person. Furthermore, those who have chosen to believe in Jesus Christ for their salvation belong to Him as members of His family. Let the following verses encourage you. If it would be helpful, write them out and put them where you can see them:

To all who received him [Jesus], to those who believed in his name,
he gave the right to become children of God.
–John 1:12

God sets the lonely in families.
–Psalm 68:6

Though my father and mother forsake me,
the LORD will receive me.
–Psalm 27:10

For we do not have a high priest who is
unable to sympathize with our weaknesses,
but we have one who has been tempted in every way,
just as we are–yet was without sin.

Let us then approach the throne of grace with confidence,
so that we may receive mercy and find grace
to help us in our time of need.
–Hebrews 4:15-16

Fear not, for I have redeemed you;
I have summoned you by name; you are mine.
–Isaiah 43:1

I don't know about you, but knowing that I have been summoned or called by God is . . . well, in the old days, I would have said "amazing." But I know enough about God's character now to know that it's not amazing that He has called us each by name. He knows us and loves us personally. So how do I finish that sentence today? Knowing God has called me by name is humbling and comforting. It reinforces that I'm deeply loved. I'm grateful for that.

Through the Father's names and Jesus' names, we can understand how we belong to Him. For example, Jesus is the Vine, Prince of Peace, Good Shepherd, Wonderful Counselor, Bread of Life, and King of Kings. Can you see how these names relate to our belongingness?

Our Response to God

I'm grateful beyond grateful that believers belong to God because of who *He* is and what *He* has done, not because of who *we* are or what we do. The only thing we have to do is believe that Jesus paid the penalty of death that our sins deserve when He died upon the cross. Because He is our Savior, we receive salvation and everlasting life in heaven. There aren't any hoops to jump through or tasks to cross off a list to try and merit this. It's a free gift!

Yet we can *choose* actions that enhance our awareness that we belong to God. These include various spiritual disciplines. We can read, study, and meditate on His powerful Word. For instance, we can become familiar with verbs describing His actions on our behalf. Looking at these verbs has enhanced my study of Scripture. David's "Song of Praise," recorded in 2 Samuel 22, is a section where the action verbs depict God's love toward us. We find, for example, that He saves, rescues, rewards, enables, and trains.

We can pray, which includes both talking to Him and listening and looking for His answers. Worship can also be a key to experiencing God's presence. I have also found that reflecting on how God is involved in my life on a day-to-day basis has been valuable. And some people benefit from keeping a journal of their prayers and reflections.

Spending quality time with others who follow Christ can also strengthen our awareness that we belong to God. Together we can study God's Word, pray, worship, and reflect on how we see God working in our lives and/or church. This is especially true when we're questioning our faith because of life's difficulties.

. . . .

REVISITING
—THE—
DYNAMIC SEQUENCE

Let's think for a moment about the dynamic sequence, applied to God this time. Belonging to God happens when our security is found in Him through a relationship with His Son, Jesus Christ. Believing in Christ alone for our salvation changes our identity. Among other things, we become children of God who are totally forgiven, deeply loved, and complete in Christ. We can consider ourselves dead to sin. Because our security and identity have shifted from lost to found, our belonging is rooted in God. Relying on God's power, believers become more like Him as they put off the sinful nature. This greatly strengthens the quality of our belonging to God because there is less in the way between Him and us. As we'll see in the next chapters, the sequence continues to lead us into purpose and competence. These, too, need to be rooted in God for us to have authentic wholeness.

If you want to belong to God and you have any doubts at all about whether you do, I hope you'll revisit chapter 3 on security and your spiritual identity list in chapter 4. Then, find a trustworthy person who can answer your questions about what it means to belong to God in Christ.

. . . .

BUILDING
—ON—
THE ROCK

▸ *Think of two or more things you're grateful for understanding about belonging.*

▸ *Which spiritual disciplines are benefiting you now? Are there some you and/or your family would benefit from practicing more faithfully? How could this come about?*

▸ *Would spending more time with certain people help you grow spiritually? Who?*

▸ *Think of two or more questions you hope I answer in the next chapter about purpose.*

▸ *Our beliefs need to be rooted in God's Word for our hope and wholeness to be authentic. Therefore, reading and meditating upon Scripture verses related to our belonging may bear fruit. You can click on the link to chapter 6 at our Web site: www.AuthenticHope.com. Among other verses, you'll see the "one anothers" listed. Not only are these very helpful to the change process, but when we live them out, we'll have a strengthened belonging. You'll also see verses related to forgiveness because this is a key concept for belonging, not just security.*

. . . .

And Jesus told His disciples:

*Come with me by yourselves to a
quiet place and get some rest.*

−Mark 6:31

SEVEN

PURPOSE
Why Am I Alive?

I HAVEN'T MET TOO MANY people who actually ask the purpose question: *Why am I alive?* Yet as we make choices, determine commitments, and set priorities, we ask and answer it all the time. People who fluctuate from one activity, college major, career, relationship, and reputation to the next, often do so because they're unsure of their reasons for living. They may be searching for what to do or who to be. They may have bought into the lie that there's something and someone who is *absolutely perfect* for them, so they keep searching. It's all wrapped up in our need to know why we exist.

For example, if we think we're alive to be powerful, our choices, commitments, and priorities will reflect that goal. We'll associate with those who can make us powerful and with those who are weaker than we are so we feel powerful. We'll spend our money and our time on activities and things that increase our power and our ability to be more powerful. We'll join prestigious clubs, even if the dues stretch our finances. We'll justify this decision because of our reason for living.

In this example:

Security: What can I trust? *My power. (Remember, this is the wrong question.)*

Identity: Who am I? *I am powerful.*

Belonging: Who wants me? *I think everyone likes it when I'm in charge. They have less to worry about.*

Purpose: Why am I alive? *To be powerful—of course!*

Competence: What do I do well? *I'm good at bossing people around.*

How we answer the purpose question is significant. The ramifications are huge. But let's not begin with purpose. Let's begin with security. If we are secure in God, through faith in Jesus Christ, and our need for identity and belonging is met through our relationship with Him, then we'll expect our purpose to also be found in Him.

Our purpose can't be met in the Ps—power, position, pleasure, possessions, popularity, pursuits—or in any other letter of the alphabet. Except maybe the letter G. Our purpose is to glorify God. That's why we're alive. We read this truth in Isaiah 43:7. We were created for God's glory.

When the noun *purpose* is signed in American Sign Language, it's done to represent a person turning around. Have we turned around? Have we turned from going through the motions (feeling like a tired gerbil in the wire wheel, busy but with nothing to show for it) and turned to making a difference? Perhaps. But have we been doing things for our own glory? "Have you noticed me? Look what I accomplished!" If so, we need to turn again, don't we?

We need to turn all the way around to God. Our character, activities, and decisions need to be chosen for God and directed to Him. Perhaps you remember my childhood nickname was "Chatty Kathy." Just having this identity and knowing my strength with words wasn't enough to guarantee I'd do something with them. Realizing that my ability to speak was from God made the difference for me. I chose to give my words back to Him in service. That's when 1 Peter 4:11 became one of my theme verses: "If anyone speaks, he should do it as one speaking the very words of God."

HOPE FOR TOMORROW

As I've already demonstrated, a right foundation of the first three components is essential for our purpose to be healthy. In addition, without hope, we might as well die. Hope for our future is a prerequisite to finding our purpose, believing in it, and doing what's necessary to fulfill it. A far-off, distant, future hope isn't as effective as an up close, nearby, present hope. Young people especially have a hard time waiting for things or events that are too vague or too far removed from their current situation. This is doubly true when they're filled with despair.

When you were in high school, were you told, "These are the best years of your life!"? Imagine how students felt who didn't like school or who weren't getting along with the people around them? I've talked to teens in those situations. They want to know why to keep living if this is as good as it gets.

A lack of hope is a significant contributor to suicide thoughts and attempts, especially among young people. Some have told me they don't want to grow up. They think their parents are unhappy and dissatisfied with virtually everything. They tell me about dads who complain about their bosses, their long days, their salary, cutting the grass, and that every time they turn around someone needs money for something. Their moms complain because they have to work outside of the home and they'd rather not, they're underpaid, there's never enough time to get things done, and the house is never clean. The children and teens summarize by asking me, "Why should I grow up and be miserable? I'd rather avoid it all."

I'm also concerned because I've met people who have committed what I call intellectual suicide, emotional suicide, social suicide, and spiritual suicide. They're alive but empty inside. They've stopped setting and pursuing academic and intellectual goals. Their emotions have flatlined because they don't want to feel any more highs and lows. They've given up on most, if not all, relationships. And they've stopped believing they can hear from God or trust the church to meet their needs.

REVISITING
—THE—
DYNAMIC SEQUENCE

The linkages between purpose and the first three components in the Model are very influential. When I meet apathetic people without purpose, I wonder about and almost always ask about their belonging, identity, and security.

Security: If we don't know who we can trust, we won't get helpful input to determine our specific purpose. If we haven't learned to appropriately trust ourselves, we may second guess everything that comes to our minds and never strive for anything as a result. And most importantly, without trusting God, we'll flounder, question our existence, and not even expect to have a purpose.

Identity: If we only know our weaknesses and those qualities that get us into trouble, we won't believe we can have a positive purpose. And significantly, if we don't claim an identity in Christ, we won't know we were created to glorify God.

Belonging: If we don't know we belong to God through faith in His Son, Jesus Christ, or if we don't value this relationship, glorifying God won't interest us. And without people to love and serve through belonging relationships, glorifying God will be more difficult.

During Emily's childhood, her belonging was unhealthy, wasn't it? Yet it's also true that belonging saved her life. Her belonging to her cat, Nathaniel, that is. When Emily was sixteen and filled with despair and overwhelming emptiness, she prepared to kill herself. She sat in the middle of her bed with the means to end her life in front of her. After months of considering suicide, she was resolved to do it. Then she heard Nathaniel meow. It hit her—if she was dead, who would feed him and her other cats? Without her, they'd die. This realization kept her alive.

Competence: What about the other side of the purpose sandwich? If we don't know why we're alive, we don't need to be good at anything. Knowing our purpose should motivate us to develop competence in a number of areas. When I talk with teens, children, and adults who lack consistent character competence and/or academic competence, it's almost always due to one of two things. They either have no reason at all for developing their skills or they have a negative purpose in mind (e.g., to get their parents' attention by misbehaving, to convince adults they're not capable of more by getting bad grades).

. . . .

As we'll see in the next chapter about competence, there are other factors that contribute to a lack of competence. For example, some children, teens, and adults need to be taught skills we assume someone else has already taught them. Yet without a purpose for living, very few people are willing to invest energy in learning and applying skills to improve their situation. So besides learning skills, people need a positive answer to the purpose question: *Why am I alive?*

WHAT DOES IT MEAN TO GLORIFY GOD?

We especially glorify God when we turn around in the most ultimate way—when we turn from sin to righteousness, sinner to saint-who-sometimes-sins, lost to found, unsaved to saved. Humbling ourselves and choosing to believe that God is God and Jesus is His Son who came to die on our behalf is the best way to glorify God. That's because glorifying God involves knowing Him and having that knowledge of Him inform all we are, all we think, and all we do.

Jesus was able to say to the Father: "I have brought you glory on earth by completing the work you gave me to do" (John 17:4). The Greek word translated *glory* in this verse means to recognize God for who and what He is and to celebrate Him with praises, worship, and adoration.[1] Hopefully this will be true of us. In 2 Corinthians 3:18, believers are told we "reflect the Lord's glory" and that we're "being transformed into his likeness with ever-increasing glory." In this context, the word *glory* means to ascribe to God His full recognition.

When I speak with children about this topic, I explain that glorifying God means we make Him look good. Because of our love for Him, we want Him known, celebrated, worshiped, and praised. I explain that glorifying God has to do with getting people's eyes off themselves and onto God instead. John states it eloquently: "He [God] must become greater; I must become less" (John 3:30).

WHY SHOULD WE GLORIFY GOD?

I wonder if you've had the same experience I have. Although I totally, 100 percent believe that we get to heaven only through believing in Jesus' sacrifice on the cross for us, I've been accused of believing in a "works mentality." Since I believe that we are saved by grace, through faith (Ephesians 2:8–9), I was concerned that others drew the opposite conclusion from observing me.

When people have allowed me to probe their misunderstanding, I've determined they saw my "good works" as my attempt to be good enough to be welcomed into heaven the day I die. For example, back when I was a university professor, I volunteered as a school board member for a Christian school. Colleagues also knew I spoke at some Christian conventions without getting paid very much. It was these types of choices that caused at least some people to assume that I was trying to earn my way into heaven.

I always, always, always enjoyed setting them straight. I did what I did and I do what I do to say "thank you" to God for what He did. It's similar to saying "thanks" to the person who holds the door open for me, to the server who pours me more water, and to someone who volunteers in our office. How much more important is it to say "thanks" to the One who sent His only Son to die for me!?!? The difference can't be measured.

HOW DO WE GLORIFY GOD?

Many families have memorized Psalm 139:14. Counted cross-stitch keepsakes of this verse hang above children's cribs and beds. These words are true for both adults and children:

> *I praise you because I am fearfully and wonderfully made;*
> *your works are wonderful, I know that full well.*
> *–Psalm 139:14*

The word *wonderfully* in this verse was translated from a Hebrew word meaning "to be distinct and marked out."[2] So this phrase doesn't mean that we're, "Wow! Wonderful! Better than others!" It means we are created as unique, one-of-a-kind, unrepeatable miracles. (Smile and reread that sentence.)

What is wonderful? According to this verse, God's works are. Therefore, it is appropriate to think of ourselves as wonderful creations. To further make this point, you might also be interested to know that the word *fearfully* comes from the same Hebrew word used throughout the Old Testament for the concept that we should "fear God."[3] (Ecclesiastes 12:13: "Fear God and keep his commandments, for this is the whole duty of man.") The same feeling of awe and reverence God wants us to have for Him, He says we can and should have toward ourselves and others, as those made in His image. Wow!

How we specifically glorify God—how we make Him look good through who we are, what we think, and what we do—is unique, according to our design. Not only did He create us with purpose; He created us on purpose. We are here at His choice, with His design. We are not accidents in a meaningless society! Although all of us have the same purpose—to glorify God—we will fulfill it differently.

Dominick: A Greater Sense of Purpose
I introduced you to Dominick in chapter 2. Through Lillian's influence and many valuable experiences, he learned he could uniquely contribute to people's writing projects. This identity strengthened his belonging. And the feedback from his

trusted friends and coworkers helped him see and believe in his specific talents and gifts.

For many years now, Dominick has glorified God by assisting many people with their writing. He has helped people find words to express their thoughts. He has supported them by clarifying and reorganizing their thoughts and managing their projects to completion. He has also created documents and reports for several ministries. His help has been invaluable to many.

In the past several months, Dominick has considered whether he should stop working with other people—maybe permanently—so he can focus on creating his own materials. Although he has uniquely and beautifully glorified God in a particular way for years and enjoyed doing it, he needs to be obedient to what God is showing him now. He is willing to work with God to make the shifts necessary to carry out a new vision and purpose.

It would be wrong to allow an established, healthy, and God-honoring identity to become so rooted that it prevents us from moving forward. This almost happened with Dominick. Some of us haven't wanted him to abandon what we've come to appreciate. That's a sad example of selfishness, and it's not the way God wants us to love one another!

Although Dominick could continue with what he's doing, he explains that the decision is between good, better, and best. In Dominick's own words: "Being a follower of Jesus Christ is about service, unconditional love, and sacrifice of self in order to find true life. I know that if I am not disciplined in developing my gifts, passion, and purpose, I'm letting down not just my Lord but my people in the church and in the world who would otherwise benefit from what only I am designed to bring to life. Sounds lofty, this Esther-sort-of-thing where you sense you truly are 'raised up for just such a time as this.'"

BUILDING
—ON—
THE ROCK

On a scale of 1–10 with 1 being "none" and 10 being "tons," how much hope for tomorrow do you have? If your rating is 5 or below, what might increase your hope? Someone to speak to? Something to do? If you have lots of hope, who could you encourage?

If you struggle to find or believe in your purpose, is it because you need to shore up your security, identity, and/or belonging? What practical steps can you take?

I've defined glorifying God as "knowing Him and having that knowledge of him inform all we are, all we think, and all we do" and "making God look good." How do you react to these descriptions? How are you doing in this area? Changes to make?

In what ways are you unique and, therefore, able to glorify God uniquely?

GLORIFYING GOD:
THREE SCRIPTURAL MANDATES

Although it's true that we'll glorify God according to our unique design, there are any number of "things" God wants all His children to do, regardless of our specific gifts, talents, interests, or age. As I prayed, reflected, and worked through many long lists of things for this section, I kept returning to just three broad topics. Accomplishing them doesn't seem so overwhelming to me. And based on God's Word, I know He'll be glorified when I behave in these ways. Perhaps the commitments I've made will inspire you. Join me, or search the Scripture for what's most relevant to you at this point in your spiritual journey.

BECOMING CHRISTLIKE

Most of us tend to be competitive and we easily compare ourselves to others. When we have that need to see how we're stacking up, let's compare ourselves to Christ. This will not only keep us humble, but we'll more readily approach His character, which will greatly please and glorify Him (Romans 8:29; 1 John 3:2).

The actual journey toward Christlikeness is unique for each person. We each have different things to improve and different methods of making progress. We need to learn to be obedient to God's direction, regardless of what others are or aren't doing. For example, when I was consciously working to not interrupt people, I noticed everyone who interrupted me! Have you had similar experiences? Rather than pointing it out to them, though, I sensed God telling me He would take care of them and I should just take care of myself. I'm grateful He shared His wisdom with me.

Of course, for our character to become more like Christ's, we must know Him. (Knowledge of Christ will positively affect all the Model's components.) We need to be reading and studying relevant Bible passages and in a church where pastors teach Christ![4]

How can we know if our character is becoming more like Christ's? I tend to ask myself if I'm growing in the same ways that Jesus grew. We read in Luke 2:52 that "Jesus grew in wisdom and stature, and in favor with God and men."

Obedience is a key. Jesus was obedient—even to death on a cross (Philippians 2:8). Therefore, let's ask ourselves whether we're demonstrating more consistent obedience in both our being and our doing. Do we sin less? Do we more often do the right things with the right attitude, in the right ways, at the right time?

FULFILLING THE GREAT COMMANDMENT

It's recorded in Mark 12:28 that a teacher of the law asked Jesus, "Of all the commandments, which is the most important?" Jesus answered, giving the two most important commandments: "'Love the Lord your God with all your heart and with all your soul and with all your mind and with all your strength.' The second is this: 'Love your neighbor as yourself.' There is no commandment greater than these" (Mark 12:30–31).

Loving God is not what won me to Him. And loving God wasn't something I thought much about until a few years ago when I was led to study Joshua 23. By this point in Joshua's life, he assumed he wouldn't live much longer so he gathered together men who would follow him. Verses 6–8 contain instructions about what to do and what not to do. I still remember reading the list and thinking, "This is great! Tasks, things to check off a list!"

Then I came to verse 11: "So be very careful to love the LORD your God." I think I audibly gasped. I wasn't expecting it. I thought, *What does love have to do with anything? How am I sure if I'm doing it? This can't be checked off a list!* After reflection, God revealed the connection to me. Obedience (i.e., doing everything else on the list) is easier when we love God. Christlikeness is easier when we prioritize our love for God. Today, I choose to get in touch with my emotional responses to God's Word, His presence, and answered prayers. I know that glorifying God is not just about doing things for Jesus; it's about growing in our love for Jesus.

What about loving our neighbor? As with everything else, the ways we show love will be unique. For example, my friend Marina loves with big bear hugs and lots of laughter. Carolina loves quietly, with listening ears. Camille loves with empathy and tears. Candy loves by remembering every detail of every event we've shared. And her husband, Greer, loves by driving us everywhere. They're amazing! Aisha loves with instruction and challenging questions. Adena loves by cleaning my house! And they all love through their prayers.

Have you noticed that not everyone responds in the same way to your love? For example, it's enough for some people to hear, "I love you." Others want us to spend time with them if we love them. Some know they're loved when we buy them gifts, some want to be touched, and others want us to do things for them to demonstrate our love. Ideally, we invest in people enough to know what works best for them.[5] Sometimes members of our staff love me by spending time with me and sometimes they do it by leaving me alone! Sometimes Aisha asks me questions and other times she knows not to. I'm grateful for their discernment. (As you've read these paragraphs, have you seen how much purpose and belonging are related?)

FULFILLING THE GREAT COMMISSION

Jesus taught His disciples: "All authority in heaven and on earth has been given to me. Therefore go and make disciples of all nations, baptizing them in the name of the Father and of the Son and of the Holy Spirit, and teaching them to obey everything I have commanded you. And surely I am with you always, to the very end of the age" (Matthew 28:18–20).

God wants people to learn about Him, receive Him through faith in His Son, and grow in their knowledge of Him (e.g., John 3:16; 2 Timothy 1:9; 3:16–17). Therefore, it's more than appropriate to think about evangelizing the lost and discipling the found as ways to bring God glory. These are our privileges whether or not we're gifted in evangelism and teaching (1 Peter 3:15). And parents should certainly make them priorities with their children.[6]

Have you figured out that I was intentional in the way I ordered these three broad categories? When we become more like Christ, we'll love more. When we choose to love God and others, we'll be motivated and prepared to share our faith and to help believers grow into Christlikeness.

As we participate with God, we must remember we'll disciple and evangelize uniquely because we are unique. People might host small groups, talk with coworkers about their faith, or volunteer to take care of children so their parents can go to Bible studies.

LIFE SKILL: LOVING

As with other components of this Model, I could have chosen several life skills, like finding hope while in the middle of heartache and despair. Many great questions arise when we think about belonging: How do we fulfill our purposes by serving others? How do we discover our particular gifts and stretch beyond them to serve from our weaknesses? How, exactly, do we share our faith? How can we help people grow in their faith who are satisfied at their plateau? These, and other questions, are worthy of answers. If they're relevant for you, I pray you're motivated to learn what you can and act on your knowledge.

God led me to the life skill of loving. I resisted for a while. "God, don't we all know how to love?" It's as if I heard Him answer me, "Do you? Do you sacrifice for others?" I also asked, "Isn't there something more important than love?" To this, I sensed Him responding, "Look at your conclusions from My Word, child! Without love, so much isn't done. Prioritize it!"

We're going back to the basics. God says it best. Check out Romans 12:9–21:

Love must be sincere.
Hate what is evil; cling to what is good.
Be devoted to one another in brotherly love.
Honor one another above yourselves.
Never be lacking in zeal,
but keep your spiritual fervor, serving the Lord.
Be joyful in hope, patient in affliction, faithful in prayer.
Share with God's people who are in need.
Practice hospitality.
Bless those who persecute you; bless and do not curse.
Rejoice with those who rejoice; mourn with those who mourn.
Live in harmony with one another.
Do not be proud, but be willing
to associate with people of low position.
Do not be conceited.
Do not repay anyone evil for evil.
Be careful to do what is right in the eyes of everybody.
If it is possible, as far as it depends on you,
live at peace with everyone.
Do not take revenge, my friends,
but leave room for God's wrath, for it is written:
"It is mine to avenge; I will repay," says the Lord.
On the contrary: "If your enemy is hungry, feed him;
if he is thirsty, give him something to drink.

In doing this, you will heap burning coals on his head."
Do not be overcome by evil, but overcome evil with good.

This is a great passage to work through. You could put a plus by those things you do well and a minus by those you could improve. Also, for each "do not" statement, can you write the "do" statement? How about reviewing this passage with those people close to you in mind? Which actions could you work on together?

Several verses from 1 Corinthians 13 follow. Ask God to let you go deep with these. How are you honestly doing? Try putting your name in place of each occurrence of the words *love* and *it*. Do you have the guts? Then, set some improvement goals. Maybe you can reread it daily for a while. If it will help, you can also rewrite the "not" statements. Of course, praying won't hurt! I've seen God bring people into my path so I have to practice the type of love that isn't easy for me. He does want us to learn, doesn't He?

Love is patient,
love is kind.
It does not envy,
it does not boast,
it is not proud.
It is not rude,
it is not self-seeking,
it is not easily angered,
it keeps no record of wrongs.
Love does not delight in evil
but rejoices with the truth.
It always protects,
always trusts,
always hopes,
always perseveres.
Love never fails.
–1 Corinthians 13:4–8

BUILDING
—ON—
THE ROCK

Allow these authenticity checkpoints to help you think more about, retain, and apply what's most important from this chapter.

▸ *Based on what you read, think of two or more things you're grateful for understanding about purpose.*

▸ *What's one practical step you can take to strengthen your character? Is there a habit you need to stop and/or a behavior to add? Who can help you reach your goal?*

▸ *Does your church offer seminars or classes related to evangelism? What about discipleship? Is there someone in your family or sphere of influence you could disciple in some area? Would you benefit from being discipled? Who can help you? When and how can you approach him or her to ask for assistance?*

▸ *What, if anything, would you like to discuss with someone close to you? Is there evidence they know their purpose?*

▸ *Think of two or more questions you hope I answer in the next chapter about competence.*

▸ *Clicking on the link to chapter 7 at our Web site (www.AuthenticHope.com) will lead you to Scripture verses related to purpose.*

*All Scripture is God-breathed and is useful
for teaching, rebuking, correcting
and training in righteousness,
so that the man of God may be
thoroughly equipped for every good work.*

–2 Timothy 3:16-17

EIGHT

COMPETENCE
What Do I Do Well?

I MEDITATED OFTEN upon Proverbs 3:5 in the first months of this ministry. I mentioned it in chapter 3 when discussing security: "Trust in the LORD with all your heart and lean not on your own understanding."

No matter the topic of my speech, to remind me of this important truth I wrote two-word phrases in the upper right-hand corner of each page of notes I spoke from. On one it said *trust in.* On the next, *lean not.* This pattern continued until the last page.

I don't want my training, experience, preparation, skill, or anything else to suffocate what I know is true—I must rely on God for my competence. The same is true for you.

I carefully chose the word *competence* to describe our fifth need. When we're competent, we have the requisite qualifications or skills for our specified work or situation; we're well qualified and capable.[1] Competence is what we need. We don't need to excel and we don't need to be perfect. We do need to be who we need to be and do what we need to do. Right? Do you agree with this for yourself? Others?

DOS AND DON'TS

Developing and using our competence depends on certain factors. To facilitate our learning, I'll share these with a contrasting "do and don't" format.

Do rely on God. Don't rely on ourselves.

In today's society, not needing anybody or anything is often touted as the best of the best. The charge is: "Be self-made!" I disagree.

For many reasons, I'm glad and grateful that Celebrate Kids, Inc., has international appeal. For one thing, I like adding to my collection of eagles and nativity scenes as I travel to different countries! I thoroughly enjoy purchasing unique gifts for others. I've seen amazing buildings and experienced rich cultural events. And best of all, I've been privileged to meet some of God's great servants.

On a personal level, I benefit from these ministry trips because my confidence in God grows. When the taxi driver knows some English, it's a blessing from God. When I like the food, it's God who gets the praise! It's definitely harder to rely on myself or believe I caused something to go well when I'm in a foreign country. Yet having to go on trips to learn to rely on God isn't practical or efficient, is it? What can we do instead?

We need to dig into God's rich, accurate, relevant, and always true Word.[2] We'll get to know God's character and attributes. By learning more about who He is, we'll know more about what He can and will do. Also, we should be in the Word when things are going well and when they're not. What do we demonstrate to others if we are people who consistently depend on and search out the Word of God for "big" things and "little" things? Let's also spontaneously share relevant Scripture during our conversations with others.

If we have families, we should also read and study the Word with them. When it comes to children, whether they want us to or not, we must be obedient to God's instruction and teach them the Word (e.g., Deuteronomy 4:9–10; 6:6–9; 11:18–21). Fathers especially need to take the lead (e.g., Isaiah 38:19).

Parents can do everything in their power to motivate and train children to choose to read God's Word on their own. Pray to God that they'll want to read it, study it, apply it often, and be transformed by it. Pray they'll love it!

The more we know of God's Word and God Himself, the more we'll realize it's foolish and dangerous to depend on ourselves. Many people benefit from structured Bible classes, small groups who study Scripture together, seminars about how to study the Bible, Bible reference books and computer programs, different Bible translations that make the Word more understandable and/or fresher, etc.

We need to be people of prayer![3] We're fools if we don't ask God for His help, wisdom, strength, energy, compassion, patience, protection, etc. It's God in us that allows us to be competent! Let's pray and expect answers in good times and bad. It's a big mistake to rely on ourselves when things are going well and only ask for God's help when we "really need it." That's the mistake, the false thinking, the lie. We need God all the time—in good times and bad! We can learn from prayer heroes such as Esther (see Esther 4:15–5:2) and Daniel (see Daniel 2:17–23). Through studying God's Word, we can learn how and why to talk with God, how and why to wait for His response, and how to discern His answers.

Mitch is a friend who understands the value of relying on God. Not long ago, before I left for an overseas trip, he wrote to say he'd pray. I e-mailed him back and said I'd pray God's best for him.

I was humbled when Mitch sent back an e-mail with this statement: "I am praying for God's best *in* me, and I know He will do it." That's a God-honoring prayer!

God's best in us is enough. It's all we need for competence (see John 15:5; Philippians 4:13; 2 Peter 1:3). I believe we can answer the competence question, *What do I do well?* with, "Anything and everything God asks me to do because He promises to fully equip me."

Do you have a tendency to rely on God or yourself? Where would you write your name on this scale?

Relying on God   Relying on Myself

⟵──⟶

Do strategically train for righteousness. Don't assume it will just happen.

We pick up some things easily, don't we? Other things, however, take longer before we catch on. Without direct instruction, it's too easy to merely pretend we know how to live, when in reality, we're learning from the "school of hard knocks." If you have children, you know that they also need guidance so they don't fall into the "I'll try anything once" mind-set.

Both adults and children need positive role modeling and clear instruction from God's Word about what is right and what is wrong (e.g., *What should I do? How should I do it? Why should I do it that way? When is that principle in effect? Is there ever a time it isn't?*).

Studying God's Word will prepare us to be more competent when guiding others. This is good news for parents since they are instructed to teach their children. Other family members, teachers at Christian schools, pastors, teachers of Sunday school classes, midweek Bible clubs, children's church, youth group, and summer camp can all help, but they are not supposed to take the parents' place. Parents have a high calling to be good teachers. Therefore, they need to be all the more sure that they are deliberately seeking God's truth. And God's Word is a great motivater![4]

When we find our children or ourselves behaving in unrighteous ways, we must not give up. That's exactly what Satan wants us to do! Rather than withdrawing, we must dig in our heels and continually turn back to God and His Word, time and time again. We must be faithful to what God clearly tells us to do.

Tackling this subject is beyond the scope of this book, but I hope you're motivated to ask questions of people you know. Maybe you're the one who can get a helpful program started at your church. You can also check out suggestions at the link for chapter 8 on our Web site: www.AuthenticHope.com.

How strategic have you been in training for righteousness? Where does your name belong on the scale below?

Strategically Training
for Righteousness

Not Training
for Righteousness

<--->

Do use godly counsel. Don't be too independent.

God wants us to rely on Him *and* to seek godly counsel. For example, Proverbs 15:22 says, "Plans fail for lack of counsel, but with many advisers they succeed." We need to ask people to help us live righteously. When thinking something through or when faced with significant decisions and problems to solve, it is foolish to act alone.

Other people's ideas will almost always stimulate more of our own. Not everyone thinks like we do, but others' critiques of our ideas will help us consider new angles. Godly counsel can result in different ideas and a more thorough analysis of what we came up with.

There are keys to implementing godly counsel. First, we need to be careful whom we ask for advice. The counsel should be from godly people, mature in their faith so they can rightly discern the situation and share ideas that line up with God's Word. We may want to include people who have experience in the issues involved. These people will offer critiques and corrections, not criticisms. Have you ever sought counsel from only those people you knew would agree with you? It's more mature to ask people who may disagree with you. They'll ask tough questions others might not. Has anyone come to your mind?

Second, we need to tell these selected people the complete truth. Have you ever been tempted to share only some details or lie a bit, hoping you'll then get the input you want? This allows you to go ahead and do what you wanted to do in the first place! But you feel better about it, don't you? For a while, anyway.

Third, we need to be willing to accept people's counsel. We can't just go through the motions. We must be humble and teachable. Rather than quickly rejecting ideas, we can ask people to clarify and elaborate.

Fourth, let's remember that it's most important to seek God's wisdom directly from Him. Getting input from His people should supplement praying and reading His Word. Some people who are very relational may have a tendency to get opinions from many people while neglecting to spend time with God. We need to guard ourselves against this.

We also may have the opportunity to be a source of godly counsel for others. How are you doing in this area? Are others free to ask you questions? Do you create windows of opportunity for discussion?

Parents, do you make time to talk with your kids about current events, politics, Scripture, school, and your day? During Jesus' teaching ministry, He was a master at this! Where would you place your names on this scale?

Using Godly Counsel	Seeking Ungodly Counsel	Being Too Independent

◄───►

Do compare ourselves to our former selves. Don't unwisely compare ourselves to others.

We'll always be able to find people who are better than us at any number of things. (If we can't, it's evidence of pride.) Choosing to compare ourselves to them can encourage us to strive for more of what God has for us. But, these comparisons can also be discouraging.

Our comparisons must be realistic. For example, if we play basketball in a community league, it may be healthy for us to compare ourselves to teammates and some players from opposing teams. It's most likely unhealthy to compare ourselves to professional ballplayers. Just as when hope is too far off in the distance, if role models are too far removed from our current skill level, discouragement can set in.

When being complimented at work, do you immediately wonder if any of your coworkers were also complimented? When your supervisor suggests you could improve in an area, do you defend yourself (either to your supervisor or just in your head) as being better than someone else? When your spouse brings up an area of concern, is your immediate reaction to talk about people with bigger problems? These reactions, and others like them, tell us whether we're comparing ourselves to our former selves or to others.

Comparing ourselves to siblings can be especially daunting. No matter our ages, these comparisons can escalate sibling rivalry. We can be motivated to change simply to be better than a sibling and/or to get more of our parents' attention. We can resent those we should hold near and dear to our hearts. Comparing ourselves to siblings can begin when we're young and continue even after our parents die. It's not healthy. The "better" siblings can resent their position and the pressure. As a result, they may choose to achieve less. And since we're not designed by God to be our sibling, we may never achieve what we think we want. Discouragement and further resentment can set in.

Whether it's bowling, managing our temper, writing more complete reports, keeping the clutter to a minimum, or something else going on in our lives, a written record can help us compare ourselves to our former selves instead of to others. I know someone who takes pictures of her kitchen and living room every Friday night. She compares these to last week's pictures and hopes to find fewer things out of place in the most recent ones. This proof helps her either be satisfied with her growth (even if her home still isn't as clutter free as her mom's) or to be realistically discouraged if she didn't make progress. The pictures also help her set realistic goals. When she relied on her memory for what her house looked like last week, she couldn't see her progress and she was constantly discouraged. We could keep a list of old bowling scores and copies of old reports to compare to current performances. We could make a note of every time our temper gets the best of us and compare today to yesterday and this week to last week. Honestly looking back on our past can be very healthy when our motivation is to improve in the future.

Where would you write your name on the scale below?

Comparing Myself   Unwisely Comparing
to My Former Self   Myself to Others

◄───►

Do work to develop competence. Don't expect perfection.

If our goal is perfection, we'll be regularly disappointed. No one can be completely accurate, without defect, all the time.[5] If we expect perfection, we may despair and not try to do anything for God because we believe the lie that we're not good enough. We may give up and not even believe in our natural talents anymore.

Many children I've talked with think their parents want them to be perfect. They say, "My parents are never satisfied. They tell me to improve and I do. I go from an 84 to a 90. They don't even say 'good' or 'thank you.' They just say, 'You can do better.'" Sometimes these kids add, often with a look of horror on their faces, "What makes them think I can do better? What happens if I can't?" When I ask these children if they believe they're unconditionally loved, the answer is almost always a no.

Rather than perfection, our goal should be to improve ourselves so we are who we need to be. Setting out to accomplish the purpose of glorifying God can motivate us. And when we're able to discover some specific ways to glorify Him, we'll be even more motivated.

Hours before planning to work on this chapter, I received an e-mail from a missionary friend in Southeast Asia. She described a mutual friend's participation in a school Easter assembly:

> I knew Anna was a dancer but I hadn't really seen her *dance*. I'd seen her do small pieces with the kids but not something where she was ministering out of her gifting and it was so impacting. I got really teary and thought how beautiful it was to see someone doing exactly what God made them/wired them to do. When they function in the gifting He has given them, they are doing what they are made to do and it can only reveal who *He* is . . . I was also reminded about how important it is to craft and hone the giftings God has given us. Anna was so impactful not just because she is a gifted dancer but because she has honed and sharpened and disciplined that gift.

Let's commit to do what it takes to develop the competencies we need to glorify God. And let's help others do the same. What areas are relevant? Character competence? Academic competence? Attitude competence? Athletic competence? Love competence? Artistic competence? Intellectual competence? Decision-making competence? Obedience competence? You get the idea. In addition to relying on God, who and what can help?

Our ministry subscribes to almost twenty monthly or bimonthly magazines and journals. Not only do we receive notices to renew these, but we regularly receive invitations to subscribe to others. I consistently toss those. After reacting in this typical manner to one invitation, I immediately knew I was wrong. I dug the card out of my wastebasket, directed our bookkeeper to subscribe, and I'm glad I did.

I remember asking myself, as I tossed the invitation to *Pray!* magazine, "Who needs an entire magazine devoted to prayer?" After tossing it, it hit me. I do! Rather than every magazine and journal relating to what I'm already passionate about, I knew I needed to expand our resource library and include *Pray!* Now I look forward to every issue. My confidence in God and prayer have increased.

I'm grateful God prompted me to subscribe to *Pray!* I almost let my past patterns control my present and future. What about you? Are you missing anything good God has for you because it's not a comfortable fit with your past or current situation? Where would you write your name on the scale below?

Not Developing Competence	Developing Competence	Expecting Perfection

$\longleftrightarrow$

Do use your competence. Don't waste your competence.

I ache for people who haven't tapped into their competence. I grieve even more for those who know their areas of competence, but choose not to use their gifts and talents. Some of them tell me, "There are plenty of people already serving." Others tell me they want to do something new and different. When I probe, I discover this "something else" is often out of their reach or something they perceive as being more glamorous than what they could easily do. But because they don't have skills for this "something else," they end up doing nothing.

I know people who talk about their competence rather than using it. "I could lead worship, too, but I'll just let Cecy serve." I've also heard, "In my last church, I was very involved with the teens. I mentored several. I've been told I'm missed." Proverbs 14:23 comes to mind: "All hard work brings a profit, but mere talk leads only to poverty."

Have you met people who haven't done what they could do because they've allowed an area of weakness to block their strength? This also saddens me. One of my weaknesses is spelling. Since I'm not very "picture smart," I can't remember what some words are supposed to look like. I depend upon the spell-check feature of my word processing program, my online dictionary, and proofreaders. Yet I know that I'm "word smart," which helped me earn a Ph.D. and write a book. We must believe enough in our strengths to use them, regardless of our weaknesses.

I know people who rest on their laurels. How sad! I know others who are always looking for new ways to serve God. Joyce and Toni, two members of our Celebrate Kids, Inc., staff, are nurses by training. They've commented that many skills they used when nursing have served them well when working with me. For example, Toni, our scheduling director, keeps detailed and accurate records. She also makes many accurate diagnoses of situations, even though she's not analyzing patients' health. The thinking pattern she learned when nursing serves her well here. It's the same way with her pleasant personality and superb people skills. It would have been very sad and wasteful if Joyce and Toni had stopped using their talents and skills just because they decided to leave their first profession.

What's the bottom line? We must be good stewards of what God has given us!

Have you allowed God to use your competence or is it going to waste?

Using Competence   Wasting Your Competence

◄───────────────────────────────────►

. . . .

BUILDING
—ON—
THE ROCK

Since you've been doing evaluations with the scales I've included, I have just two questions for you to ponder before you continue reading. Let's compare followers of the Lord Jesus Christ to those who haven't accepted Him as Savior. How do you think competence is different? And secondly, what are some possible results of the differences?

. . . .

Dominick: Illustrating the Principles

Dominick is one of my heroes, in part, because he exemplifies every one of these competence "do" statements. In chapter 7, I wrote that Dominick was "willing to work with God to make the shifts necessary to carry out a new vision and purpose." How did Dominick get to this point? He would say, "I've experienced God at every stage of my life, so why wouldn't He be faithful in the next?"

How does Dominick know he is "raised up for just such a time as this"? Godly counsel played a part. He willingly invited trusted friends and colleagues to help him think about his future. He not only sent out prayer updates, but he also asked if we had wisdom for him, especially regarding a potential move across country and shift in his responsibilities.

As long as I've known Dominick, he has compared himself to his former self. Personal growth is one of his integrity goals. We have also talked about how he specifically compares to certain people in related fields. I've noticed that he doesn't desire to stand out in a crowd. In fact, just the opposite is true. He'd be fine if more people were wired like him. Our discussions increased Dominick's understanding of the uniqueness of his combination of abilities, understandings, and passions. That isn't prideful; it's a statement of fact. Knowing his strengths fuels his desire to develop whatever skills are necessary to do what he needs to do.

That's good, since things didn't turn out as he expected after his move. Rather than spending all his time writing, he was led to spend time learning how to best package and deliver his ideas. Therefore, he's going to conferences he didn't expect to. He's spending money on computer software he didn't know he'd need. Dominick, who already knows a lot and has contributed to society in many ways, is humbling himself to spend months learning. He doesn't think of it as a sacrifice. He knows it's necessary to develop competencies God wants him to have.

The Carlton Family: Living the Dynamic Sequence

I think a slice-of-life illustration from Reeve, Brooke, Jackson, and their extended family provides a beautiful example of how competent parenting led to a son's competence remaining intact. In fact, because of a certain incident, all five components of the Model could have been destroyed for Reeve and his parents, and none of them were. To God be the glory!

Jackson and Brooke parent Reeve and his brothers well. They definitely rely on God and live out the other "do" statements from this chapter. They get along well and they regularly communicate. I thank God for the firm foundation Reeve had when the world came tumbling down around him.

I hadn't talked with Jackson for a while, so I was surprised to hear from him. He wanted to fill me in on something involving Reeve, in case I had advice and so I could pray. With passion that surprised me, he commented, "You know, Kathy, I'm not highly emotional except when it comes to my kids. Nobody should mess with my kids!"

Reeve was accused of doing something in school that he didn't do. Yet because of school policies and the other family's response to the incident, Reeve was punished as if he had done "it." (Reeve made a mistake that led to the false accusation. He's always understood that and willingly owned this piece of the problem.)

Reeve's entire family responded beautifully. For example, since Jackson was out of town, both of Reeve's grandfathers attended a meeting with Brooke and an administrator. Not only did Brooke appreciate their support, but Reeve also learned his grandfathers' love and support ran deep. And the administrator knew Reeve had a family!

Jackson flew home early from his international business trip. This made quite a statement. He came home because he's Reeve's dad, not because he didn't trust Brooke. He knew he needed to be there and sacrificed to put his son first. Both of Reeve's older brothers called regularly to offer support and to make sure Reeve knew they didn't believe the accusation. Reeve told his parents he didn't know they cared that much. Sometimes it takes a crisis, doesn't it?

Jackson and Brooke increased their presence at Reeve's school. They made sure the administrators knew they had their support, but that they'd also be observing to make sure Reeve was treated fairly. By observing his parents, Reeve learned more about standing up for himself.

Jackson and Brooke kept parenting in the midst of the turmoil. They were there for each other and for Reeve. They continually told him he was "a good kid." They provided role modeling and instruction. They requested prayer support. They sought guidance from trustworthy and knowledgeable Christians. They helped Reeve understand why this happened and how to avoid similar situations.

Before this incident, Reeve had competence and an excellent sense of where it came from. He still does because the other components remained strong. As a result of the situation, he also has more security in his family. No doubt self-security in-creased too. Immediately after the accusation, his security prob-ably diminished. But because of Reeve's family's response and the numerous conversations he had with his parents, it's healthy again. His belonging to his family is also enhanced. And because of professional educators and good friends who didn't believe his accuser, his belonging at school hasn't suffered permanent damage. I praise God that Reeve's teachers consid-ered his exemplary record of behavior and believed that identi-ty rather than the one he was accused of having.

Reeve's identity remains "I'm a good kid" when it could have quickly turned to "I'm a troublemaker," or worse. His purpose remains to glorify God, when it could have easily changed to getting revenge. The role modeling of his parents was significant! All five of Reeve's needs remain met in healthy ways, unlike in some families where one incompetent act caus-es the entire Model to fold.

I haven't mentioned God in this illustration from Reeve's life. Do you think his view of God was influenced by what happened? If so, how? What about his parents' view of God?

LIFE SKILL: DECISION MAKING

As with other components, there are several life skills for compe-tence. I've chosen the skill of decision making because we make hun-dreds of decisions each week—maybe each day! Do you agree that when a decision turns out well, you feel good deep down? That's the feeling of competence. Not only is decision making very linked to competence; it's also essential to self-security. When our decision-making compe-tence grows, we can more readily trust ourselves. In this significant way, competence and security are linked.

Therefore, talk with others about your decision-making process. Think out loud sometimes so they can hear what you're thinking. This can help them learn cause-effect reasoning. In other words, rather than just verbalizing decisions you come to after analyzing the situation, ver-balize your analysis too. It might sound something like this:

We're going to be late for church again. We're going to have to do something different next Wednesday night. How should I handle it when we're finished with dinner? I could tell everybody to take their plates to the sink, but I know they'll whine. I guess we could leave everything on the table, but by the time we get back, the spaghetti sauce will be stuck on good, making it much harder to clean. That's not a good idea. And some of the dishes could permanently stain. Ruth is finished. I think I'll have her go and get my Bible, purse, keys, and jacket. Then I'll be ready to go. While she's doing that, I can supervise the clean up. Each kid can rinse their own plate and then go get their stuff. I think that will be quicker than having JJ do them all, even though it's his night. Maybe I shouldn't assign Wednesday night to anyone from now on. It will be everybody's night . . .

When people you know make wise decisions, tell them. In other words, rather than saying the generic and unhelpful "Good job," say, "You made a wise choice," or "Your decision was smart," or "You thought that through completely, considered lots of relevant truth, and came up with a smart decision. I'm impressed!" This growing identity of "smart decision maker" can help them the next time they're faced with making a choice.

Within reason, allow others to suffer the consequences of bad decisions. Don't always bail people out. Some examples of this with children are: If Veronica decides to make noise while others are watching a video, she must leave the room. If Adrian doesn't put his bike away, he loses the privilege of riding it the next day. If MaiSee chooses to lie, her word will be checked constantly until she has proven herself trustworthy again. Let children and adults know that, through their behavior, they *choose* their consequences. It's not that they're being punished.

Decision making is only as good as the information we have. Therefore, we need to know how to access accurate, detailed, and relevant information.If you know this has tripped you up before, check out the suggestions at the chapter 8 link on our Web site: www. AuthenticHope.com. Also, if you think in terms of the people you can rely on for information, this aspect of competence links to security and belonging, doesn't it?

When faced with making a decision, these questions and steps may help:

- Is it a moral decision (a matter of right versus wrong)? If it is, do what's right, in the right way, at the right time, with the right motives, etc. Then evaluate your experience.
- Or is it a wisdom decision (what is good versus better or best)? If it is, how will you involve rational thinking, intuition, and relationships when deciding what to do? Will you involve prayer and searching for God's wisdom in Scripture?
- List and evaluate your options. When evaluating, consider if each option is biblical, accurate, efficient, complete, fair to everyone, etc.
- Most options can be classified as possible as is, possible with a change, or impossible. Categorize yours.
- Now choose from among the possible options. Of those that are possible as is, what's the risk level? Of those that need changes, are the changes realistic? What's worth doing?
- Now list remaining options.
- Choose and implement your decision. Pray first, seek more godly counsel if that's appropriate, and do additional Bible study. Don't get stuck at this step! Choose and implement something.
- After implementing your decision, seek feedback and observe for feedback in yourself, others, and the situation. Are you at peace or stressed? Content or dissatisfied?
- Accept consequences. Decide what you might do differently next time.

BUILDING
—ON—
THE ROCK

What's most important from this chapter? Perhaps these authenticity checkpoints will help you discern what's most valuable to think more about, retain, and apply.

> ▸ *Based on what you read, think of two or more things you're grateful for understanding about competence.*
> ▸ *Which "Do and Don't" statement is most important for you to think more about? What's one practical step to move you toward the "do" side of the statement? Who can help you reach your goal?*
> ▸ *Would you benefit from some help with Bible study or prayer? Is there someone who can mentor you? Can you encourage your church to offer a seminar or two? Would you be willing to read a book on one of these topics?*
> ▸ *Clicking on the link to chapter 8 at our Web site (www.AuthenticHope.com) will lead you to Scripture verses related to competence. Perhaps you can study them as a family.*

*His divine power has given us every-
thing we need for life and godliness
through our knowledge of him who
called us by his own glory and goodness.*

–2 Peter 1:3

CONCLUSION

I'LL CONCLUDE THIS BOOK the way I do most seminars on authentic hope and wholeness. Some people try to use one of their competencies to also meet their security, identity, belonging, and purpose needs. This is dangerous and unhealthy. Notice this pattern begins with the wrong question. We're doomed from the beginning. For example:

> **Security:** *What* can I trust? *My writing ability.*
> **Identity:** Who am I? *I'm an author.*
> **Belonging:** Who wants me? *My readers!*
> **Purpose:** Why am I alive? *To be an author.*
> **Competence:** What do I do well? *I write well!*

Let me assure you that these are not my answers! If they were, who would I be and what would I do if no one reads this book?

Frankly, as I'm finishing what has been a true labor of love, I could answer three out of five questions similarly to how I have above. My writing competence is certainly on my mind. This book is an accomplishment, so it's understandable that I'm thinking about my new identity of "book author" rather than "magazine columnist" or other true identities. But I can't think of myself only as an author. That's way too narrow and could result in egotistical behavior on my part. More importantly, the answers above leave God out of the equation.

What do I change? I have to change the security question, which will force me to change its answer. Which other one will change? I cannot answer the purpose question in the same way ("To be an author"). My new answer will refocus everything else. When we identify what to change, it can reorient everything!

What's my purpose? I'm alive to glorify God! It appears He is allowing me to do this, in part, through the writing of this book. It's a discipleship tool, and God has used the Model to bring many into His family. Therefore, it also fulfills the purpose of evangelism. I'm grateful beyond grateful He is allowing me the privilege of challenging you with this Model! Here are some of my answers:

Security: Who can I trust? *The triune God—all the time, for everything. This includes trusting Him to equip me.*

Identity: Who am I? *I'm someone Jesus died for. I'm also more of an influencer now since God has allowed me to write a book.*

Belonging: Who wants me? *God does. Hopefully readers of my book will connect with me. I don't need them to, but I hope they will because it will make reading the book a better experience for them.*

Purpose: Why am I alive? *To glorify God through all I am and in all I do. This includes writing but is not limited to that.*

Competence: What do I do well? *Because of God's wisdom and strength, insights from the Holy Spirit, and mentoring, I've learned to write better.*

How would you answer these life-changing questions? Writing down answers that are currently accurate might be an excellent way for you to conclude this experience.

Do you know anyone who might answer the questions this way:

Security: What can I trust? *My looks.*
Identity: Who am I? *A beautiful blond with great skin.*
Belonging: Who wants me? *My mom, dad, and boyfriend when I'm beautiful.*
Purpose: Why am I alive? *To be the most beautiful of all.*
Competence: What do I do well? *I look great. My hair is perfect.*

Who will this person be (and what will she be like) when she has a bad hair day? She'll have nothing! She asked the wrong first question, so it set a dangerous pattern.

And here's a scenario that's far too common. I'll honor my grandfather by using his name in the illustration. He was mayor of my city when I was a child and he remains one of my heroes.

Security: Who can I trust? *Ervin.*
Identity: Who am I? *Ervin's date.*
Belonging: Who wants me? *Ervin does.*
Purpose: Why am I alive? *To get Ervin to love me.*
Competence: What do I do well? *I love Ervin. I make him happy.*

What happens to the girl answering these questions on the days Ervin won't even look in her direction? She has nothing! We can't allow our children or ourselves to expect *anything* or any one person to meet all our needs, unless that person is God.

Security: Who can I trust? *The triune God.*
Identity: Who am I? *Someone Jesus died for!*
Belonging: Who wants me? *God does. He always will!*
Purpose: Why am I alive? *To glorify God in all I am, think, and do.*
Competence: What do I do well? *Anything God asks me to do in His power, strength, wisdom, and love.*

Please note that the answer to the last question is especially relevant if you're wondering if you can apply what you've learned about this Model. I imagine you've been applying ideas here and there, as you've seen the Model work in your everyday world. In that way, you're already successful. As you're open to God's leadership, He will show you what's most relevant for you. Then He will fully and beautifully equip you to apply it. Absolutely! Praise God!

NOTES

Chapter 1: Rock Bottom or Anchored to the Rock?

1. Garth Baker-Fletcher, *Somebodyness: Martin Luther King Jr., and the Theory of Dignity* (Minneapolis: Fortress Press, 1993).

Chapter 2: Chutes and Ladders Linkages

1. We used an activity-based program titled *Building Self-Esteem* by Robert W. Reasoner (Consulting Psychologists Press, Inc., 1982). Although Reasoner positioned the five components in his three-ring binder in the same order I do, he didn't explain that the order is important. Although this was a secular program and had some deficiencies, I'm grateful for it because God used it to stimulate my thinking and begin my study and research into people's core needs.

2. I now present this material regularly to teachers, parents, and students of all ages in public school programs and at conventions. Because I've spent time and put forth effort to see the triune God in the Model of Authentic Hope and Wholeness, it's not as frustrating for me now to teach this material in secular settings. God has shown my associate speakers and me how we can present this appropriately and legally so it's still very positive and empowering.

Chapter 3: Security: Who Can I Trust?

1. Please visit our Web site, www.AuthenticHope.com, for a list of Scriptures you can study for yourself to see how they support this and other statements from this chapter. Just click on the link for chapter 3.

2. Among the best material available about forgiveness is June Hunt's *Forgiveness: Forgiving When You Don't Feel Like It* (2004). It is one of her printed resources in the *Biblical Counseling Keys* she has developed. You can order it at www.hopefortheheart.org or by calling 1-800-488-HOPE. Their address is: Hope for the Heart, PO Box 7, Dallas, TX 75221.

Chapter 4: Identity: Who Am I?

1. For a list of relevant Scripture and excellent books, newsletters, and Web sites that address our identity in Christ, visit our Web site: www.AuthenticHope.com. Click on the link for chapter 4.

Chapter 5: The Change Process

1. I've posted the change process I used for impatience on our Web site, along with other examples, to further assist you in persevering through change to Christlike and God-honoring behavior. In fact, I shared my interrupting example with Camille, a longtime friend. When we talked, she said it helped her realize her own interrupting habit, but that some of her reasons were different. She willingly has allowed me to post her process on our Web site. It will help you understand there's no one right reason, conclusion, or verse. You'll find these by clicking on the link for chapter 5 at www.AuthenticHope.com.

2. Kathy Collard Miller, *The Useful Proverbs* (Grand Rapids: World Publishing, 1997). Ray Pritchard, *The ABC's of Wisdom: Building Character with Solomon* (Chicago: Moody, 1997).

3. John G. Kruis, *Quick Scripture Reference for Counseling*, 3rd ed. (Grand Rapids: Baker, 2000).

4. Hope for the Heart, www.hopefortheheart.org, 1-800-488-HOPE.

5. You may enjoy searching for the "one-another" instructions in the New Testament, and I encourage you to do that. However, if busyness makes this unrealistic now, you can go to our Web site (www.AuthenticHope.com) and click on the link to chapter 5 to find a list of the "one-another" verses.

6. True guilt is a consequence of sin (e.g., Leviticus 5:17; 2 Samuel 24:10; James 2:10). Guilt is a fact, not a feeling. When we repent and pray to God, confessing our sin and choosing to turn from it and to Him, we're forgiven and the guilt is lifted (e.g., Psalms 32:5; 103:12; 1 John 1:9). Have you heard the term *false guilt*? It's based on self-condemning feelings. Have you ever continued to blame yourself after you've confessed sin? Have you ever blamed yourself when you haven't done anything wrong? False guilt is rooted in lies and false beliefs. If allowed to fester, it's horribly stifling and damaging at many levels. Perhaps it's what God would want you or people you know to "put off." Working through June Hunt's Biblical Counseling Key called *Guilt: Living Guilt Free* (2003) could facilitate your healing process. It's brilliant! See www.hopefortheheart.org for this resource.

Chapter 6: Belonging: Who Wants Me?

1. I have many dreams about school- and church-based education. Imagine teaching friendship skills with the same intentionality that we teach reading, writing, and math. For instance, even though all friendship skills are relevant to people of all ages, what if we assigned the teaching of certain skills to certain grades? By the time children entered middle school, they could have a firmly established and accurate set of friendship skills to rely upon. Wow! (If you ever take this ball and run with it, please send me a list of your skills and how you'd assign them to various grades. I'd benefit from your insights!)

2. For more about these levels see June Hunt's Biblical Counseling Key called *Friendship: Iron Sharpening Iron* (2003). See www.hopefortheheart.org more information.

Chapter 7: Purpose: Why Am I Alive?

1. Spiros Zodhiates, ed., *The Complete Word Study Dictionary: New Testament,* rev. ed. (Chattanooga: AMG Publishers, 1993).

2. R. Laird Harris, ed., *Theological Wordbook of the Old Testament,* vol. 2 (Chicago: Moody, 1980).

3. Warren Baker, ed., *The Complete Word Study Dictionary: Old Testament* (Chattanooga: AMG Publishers, 1994).

4. Please visit our Web site, www.AuthenticHope.com for a list of suggestions. Just click on the link for chapter 7.

5. Are you familiar with the five love languages, as described by Dr. Gary Chapman? If you are, apply your understanding here. If you're not, you should be. You'll truly benefit. More importantly, those you love will benefit. We're naturally wired by God to enjoy love that is expressed in certain ways: physical touch, words of affirmation, quality time, gifts, or acts of service. Loving others means putting them first and communicating our love in ways that are best for them, even if it's a stretch for us. For example, physical touch isn't all that important to me, but it is to my friend Marina. Therefore, I willingly hug her, rub her shoulder when I'm communicating something important, and even tussle her hair on occasion. I recommend you read at least one of Gary's books:

   Gary Chapman, *The Five Love Languages,* rev. ed. (Chicago: Northfield, 2005).

   Gary Chapman, *The Five Love Languages for Singles* (Chicago: Northfield, 2005).

   Gary Chapman, *The Five Love Languages: Men's Edition,* rev. ed. (Chicago: Northfield, 2004).

   Gary Chapman, *The Five Love Languages of Teenagers* (Chicago: Northfield, 2000).

   Gary Chapman and Ross Campbell, M.D., *The Five Love Languages of Children* (Chicago: Northfield, 1997).

   Gary Chapman, *Five Signs of a Loving Family* (Chicago: Northfield, 1997).

6. I pray that more parents will realize that one of their primary purposes is to raise children to know, love, serve, and glorify God. My friend Connie Neal has written an excellent book to help us raise and educate children during these challenging days. Her emphasis on the Word of God is outstanding. It's what we need in order to glorify God. I highly recommend her book: Connie Neal, *Walking Tall in Babylon: Raising Children to Be Godly and Wise in a Perilous World* (Colorado Springs: Waterbrook, 2003).

Have you thought about writing purpose and mission statements for yourself and your family? For example, my church's mission is "developing functioning followers of Christ."

Chapter 8: Competence: What Do I Do Well?

1. Lesley Brown, ed., *The New Shorter Oxford English Dictionary on Historical Principles,* 5th ed. (New York: Oxford University Press, 1993). *Webster's New World Dictionary & Thesaurus,* 4th ed., CD-Rom (Renton, Wash.: TOPICS Entertainment, 2003).

2. When clicking on the link for chapter 8 at our Web site, you'll find recommended resources for Bible study. I'll share some methods with you too. For example, have you ever read Psalm 23 several times in a row? Read it once paying attention to the personal pronouns, another time for the places and their order, and a third time for the action verbs associated with the Shepherd. What do you see that you haven't seen before?

3. For some of my favorite resources about prayer, click on the link for chapter 8 at our Web site: www.AuthenticHope.com. You'll also find Bible verses that motivate me to pray and methods I use.

4. Connie Neal, in her excellent book, *Walking Tall in Babylon: Raising Children to Be Godly and Wise in a Perilous World* (Colorado Springs: Waterbrook, 2003), points out that God includes fear motivation (e.g., Deuteronomy 32:47), love and hope motivation (e.g., Deuteronomy 5:29), reward motivation (e.g., Deuteronomy 28:1–14), and duty motivation (e.g., Deuteronomy 4:10; 6:7; 11:19–21; Ephesians 6:4). *Walking Tall* will help you train children. I highly recommend it.

5. Brown, ed., *The New Shorter Oxford English Dictionary. Webster's New World Dictionary & Thesaurus.*

INDEX